CLASSICAL EPIC: HOMER AND VIRGIL

Current and forthcoming titles in the Classical World Series

Classical World Series

CLASSICAL EPIC: HOMER AND VIRGIL

Richard Jenkyns

Bristol Classical Press

General Editor: John H. Betts
Series Editor: Michael Gunningham

This impression 2004
First published in 1992 by
Bristol Classical Press
an imprint of
Gerald Duckworth & Co. Ltd.
90-93 Cowcross Street, London EC1M 6BF
Tel: 020 7490 7300
Fax: 020 7490 0080
inquiries@duckworth-publishers.co.uk
www.ducknet.co.uk

A catalogue record for this book is available
from the British Library

ISBN 1 85399 133 3

Printed and bound in Great Britain by
Antony Rowe Ltd

Contents

List of Illustrations

Preface

This book is about three poems, the *Iliad*, the *Odyssey* and the *Aeneid*. There are many sides to these works, and no one will expect a full and balanced account of them all in so short a compass; my aim has been to give some idea of why the poems deserve to be studied, admired and enjoyed. Given the scope of the book, it has seemed sensible to look at the *Odyssey* particularly in the light of the *Iliad* and Virgil in the light of Homer.

The Classical World series is designed to be usable by readers who have no knowledge of the classical languages and perhaps only a brief acquaintance with the ancient world. I myself like to read books on subjects about which I know little or nothing, but I do not care to be patronised, and I have written for readers who feel the same. So although I have avoided technicalities, or if need be explained them, I have not gone out of my way to make this an easy book; I hope that it may be interesting to those who know the classics well, and even to experts. I have tried to write for anyone at all who takes pleasure in these poems or wants to know something about them.

Readers should also be warned that though some of the assertions in the book would command wide agreement, others are novel or controversial. There are several reasons for this. I do not like 'highest common factor' books; in any case, it is not easy to say much about Homer or Virgil that someone will not disagree with, and a book limited to facts and truisms would be unbearably dull. But above all, these great poems ask for the personal, imaginative engagement of each reader; there is a sense in which a book of truths universally acknowledged, by its very blandness, would give the falsest impression of all.

For quotations from the *Iliad*, unless otherwise stated, I have used Martin Hammond's translation, published by Penguin; I have however Latinised the spelling of proper names, so that the same figures do not appear in different guises in different parts of the book; thus Achilles for Achilleus, Ajax for Aias, Hector for Hektor, and so on. I have made my own translations of the *Odyssey* and *Aeneid*; these aim simply to be literal and make no pretence at elegance whatever.

I am grateful to Martin Hammond and Penguin Books for allowing me to quote from his translation of the *Iliad*. Warm thanks also, for help and advice of various kinds, to Anne Bowtell, Michael Gunningham and Ian Jenkins. My debt is of course very large to all those who have taught me about Homer and Virgil, by word of mouth and on the printed page.

R.H.A.J.

Dates and Authorship

HOMER: The problem of the authorship of the *Iliad* and the *Odyssey* is discussed in the first chapter. The poems are likely to have originated in the islands of the eastern Aegaean Sea or in what is now the western coast of Turkey. Dating is very uncertain: a reasonable hypothesis is that the *Iliad* came to something like its present form in the last third of the eighth century BC, the *Odyssey* between twenty and forty years later.

VIRGIL (Publius Vergilius Maro, 70-19 BC) was born near Mantua. From his early thirties he was under the patronage of Maecenas, who was charged by Caesar Octavian (later the Emperor Augustus) with collecting a circle of poets who would add lustre to Caesar's name and achievements. Virgil's earlier works were the *Eclogues*, a collection of ten poems mostly on pastoral themes, and the *Georgics*, a work in four books which explores his feelings about Italy and the life of the countryside through the medium of a didactic poem on agriculture (arable farming, the cultivation of vines and trees, the care of livestock, and bee-keeping). He is likely to have begun the *Aeneid* in the early 20s BC. At his death he left the poem with some lines unfinished and the whole unrevised.

The Plots

The Troy Story

All three poems are related to the story of Troy. Paris, son of Priam,
king of Troy, was invited to judge which was the most beautiful of
three goddesses, Hera, Athena and Aphrodite (Latin names: Juno,
Minerva, Venus). He chose in favour of Aphrodite, goddess of love,
in return for which she enabled him to seduce Helen, wife of
Menelaus, king of Sparta, and take her to Troy. To avenge this insult,
Troy was besieged by a Greek army led by a federation of chieftains
under the overall command of Menelaus' brother, Agamemnon, king
of Mycenae. (Troy is also called Ilium – hence *Iliad*.)

The Iliad

The *Iliad* has one of the best plots ever devised. Its outlines are simple,
but there is a very large cast of subsidiary characters. The essential
plot is given here; added in brackets are some details or episodes
which may clarify the discussion in this book.

It is the tenth and last year of the war. The Trojan priest of
Apollo offers ransom for the return of his daughter, who is
Agamemnon's captive. Agamemnon insults him, and the god Apollo
sends a plague on the Achaean (i.e. Greek) army. The Achaean
chieftains meet: Agamemnon agrees to return the girl, but angered
by the speech of Achilles, son of Peleus, the best of the Achaean
warriors, seizes Achilles' own captive woman, Briseis. Achilles with-
draws from battle and appeals for help to his mother, the sea-goddess
Thetis. (We learn that his life is destined to be short.) She prevails on
Zeus, king of the gods, to give the Trojans the upper hand in the battle,
so that the Achaeans will have to make terms with Achilles.

Under the leadership of Hector, son of King Priam, the Trojans
begin to gain the upper hand. (Hector's wife Andromache, with their
baby son, is introduced in a scene in which she talks with him before

he re-enters battle.) Agamemnon is forced to back down, and sends an embassy to Achilles (consisting of two chieftains, Ajax and Odysseus, and Achilles' old tutor, Phoenix) offering the return of Briseis and a vast recompense in addition. (Phoenix tells the story of the anger of another hero, Meleager, trying to persuade Achilles that if he delays too long, he may lose the recompense.) Achilles angrily rejects the offer, declaring that he will not do battle again until the Trojans are setting fire to the Achaean ships.

Distressed by the continued Achaean reverses, Patroclus, Achilles' intimate friend, persuades Achilles to let him enter the fight wearing Achilles' armour. (Patroclus inflicts slaughter on the Trojans and kills Sarpedon, a Lycian who is fighting with the Trojans as an ally.) Hector kills Patroclus.

Achilles is stricken with grief and rage. (Thetis persuades the god Hephaestus to make him new armour, including a shield depicting many scenes of human activity.) He now makes up his quarrel with Agamemnon, passionately eager to plunge into battle again. He kills many Trojans, and finally meets and kills Hector. To avenge Patroclus he refuses to return Hector's body for burial and attempts to mutilate it by dragging it behind his chariot (though the gods prevent the mutilation by supernatural means). Patroclus' ghost appears to Achilles, asking for burial. Achilles sacrifices animals and Trojan prisoners by his pyre. He organises funeral games, which show him in a newly humane light.

There is contention among the gods between those who favour the Achaeans and those who favour Troy, but the squabble is soon settled. The gods agree to tell Achilles to hand back Hector's corpse, and arrange for Priam (escorted by the god Hermes, disguised as a young man) to come alone to bring the ransom and collect his son. Achilles shows generosity and pity towards Priam, and a short truce is arranged for the funeral rites.

The Odyssey

Books 1-4. Ten years after the end of the Trojan War, Odysseus, king of the island of Ithaca, has still not returned home, thanks to the enmity of the sea-god Poseidon. His palace is occupied by local nobles, who are wasting his substance; they are suitors for the hand of his faithful wife Penelope, who is finding it hard to resist their demands that she choose one of them. The goddess Athena prevails on Zeus to enable Odysseus to return. She comes to Ithaca, in disguise, to put heart into Telemachus, Odysseus' son; he holds an assembly, and sets off on a journey to enquire after his father, visiting the court of Nestor at Pylos and (with Nestor's son Peisistratus) the court of Menelaus and Helen at Sparta.

Books 5-8. Meanwhile Zeus sends the messenger god Hermes to the island of Ogygia, where the amorous goddess Calypso has for years kept hold of Odysseus. She is told to let him go; he builds a raft and leaves, and after being shipwrecked in a storm sent by Poseidon is washed ashore at Scheria, land of the Phaeacians. He is rescued by the princess Nausicaa, who tells him to go to her parents, Alcinous, the Phaeacian king, and Arete. He is hospitably received, and at a feast is asked to tell his name and story.

Books 9-12. He tells his adventures, in which all his men perished. Some of them are captured by the one-eyed cannibal giant, Polyphemus the Cyclops, from whom they escape by blinding him. He is Poseidon's son; hence the god's wrath. After the Laestrygonians, another cannibal people, have destroyed eleven of Odysseus' ships and their crews, the surviving ship reaches Aeaea, island of the enchantress Circe. She turns some of Odysseus' men into pigs, but by supernatural assistance he outwits her, and they have an affair. Odysseus leaves her and comes to a place where he calls up the ghosts of the dead: the seer Teiresias foretells his future, and he also meets his mother Anticleia, Achilles, Agamemnon and his old rival Ajax. On another island they find the cattle of the Sun, which they are forbidden to touch, but driven by hunger, they kill and eat some; only Odysseus refrains. In consequence Zeus wrecks the ship, and Odysseus alone survives, cast ashore on Calypso's isle. (Other adventures include the Lotus-Eaters, Aeolus and the bag of winds, the Sirens, and Scylla and Charybdis.)

Books 13-20. The Phaeacians leave Odysseus on Ithaca, asleep. He meets Athena, disguised again, and tries to deceive her with a lying story. She reveals herself, promises help, and disguises him as an aged beggar. He is hospitably received by the loyal swineherd Eumaeus, to whom he tells more false tales about himself. Telemachus returns, accompanied by a seer, Theoclymenus, whom he has met on the journey, and escapes a plot by the suitors to kill him. He comes to Eumaeus' hut, and Odysseus reveals his identity to him. Odysseus,

Eumaeus and Telemachus come to the palace. The aged hound Argus recognises Odysseus, and dies. Odysseus is insulted by the goatherd Melanthius, the beggar Irus, the maidservant Melantho and several suitors. Odysseus and Penelope converse; she tells the housekeeper Eurycleia to wash him, and Eurycleia recognises him by his scar. Theoclymenus foresees the suitors' deaths from a vision of blood dribbling from their mouths as they eat meat.

Books 21-3. Penelope tests the suitors by inviting them to string Odysseus' bow and shoot through a line of axes. They fail to string the bow. Odysseus reveals himself to Eumaeus and the loyal oxherd Philoetius. He strings the bow and shoots through the axes. Odysseus, Telemachus and the two loyal herdsmen kill the suitors. Those slave-girls who were disloyal are hanged, and Melanthius is hideously mutilated. Penelope refuses to believe in Odysseus' identity. As a trick she orders his bed to be moved; Odysseus, who had built the bed around a living tree, flares up in anger, and Penelope acknowledges that this is truly her husband. They retire into the bed.

Book 24. The souls of the suitors pass to the underworld, where they meet Agamemnon and Achilles. Odysseus visits his father Laertes, who is living in decrepit conditions in the country, and after testing him with another false story, reveals himself. The suitors' kin plan vengeance; there is a skirmish, but Athena intervenes and brings peace.

The Aeneid

Book 1. Aeneas is the leader of a band of Trojans who have survived the sack of Troy. Jupiter, king of the gods, has willed that he shall go to Italy and establish the people that will ultimately found Rome; but his wife, Juno, is resolved to continue her persecution of the Trojans. Juno arranges for a storm to batter Aeneas' ships; the remnants of his fleet make landfall on the African coast, near Carthage. Jupiter reassures Aeneas' mother, the goddess Venus, and reveals the future greatness of Rome, culminating in the rule of Augustus. Aeneas meets Venus, disguised as a young huntress. The Trojans are hospitably received by the queen of Carthage, Dido, a young widow. Juno and Venus, from different motives, conspire to make Dido fall in love with Aeneas.

In *Books 2 and 3* Aeneas tells her his adventures. The Greeks sack Troy. In the confusion he loses his wife Creusa; her ghost tells him that a new wife and kingdom await him in a western land. He escapes with his father Anchises and son Ascanius. He and his followers then undergo wanderings modelled on those of Odysseus. They get guidance from visions, but at first misunderstand the command to seek their 'ancient mother' (Italy, from where Dardanus, founder of Troy, originated). In Epirus they meet another Trojan survivor, Helenus, now married to Hector's widow Andromache. Anchises dies.

Book 4. Dido's sister Anna urges her to yield to her love for Aeneas, but she resists, because she has sworn perpetual fidelity to her dead husband, Sychaeus. Juno arranges a storm while she and Aeneas are hunting; they shelter in the same cave, and their love is consummated. Dido calls their liaison a marriage. Jupiter sends Mercury to chide Aeneas for lingering in Carthage. Before Aeneas has found a good time to break the news of his departure to Dido, she finds out and upbraids him. He keeps to his resolve; as he sails away, she kills herself, having cursed the Trojans and their posterity.

Book 5. Aeneas holds memorial games for Anchises in Sicily. Anchises appears in a dream and tells him to visit him in the underworld so that he may be strengthened for the task ahead. The sea-god Neptune allows the Trojans safe passage to Italy, requiring one life as forfeit: the helmsman Palinurus is lulled magically to sleep and falls overboard.

Book 6. At Cumae Aeneas meets the Sibyl, a prophetess. With her as guide, he enters the underworld, meets Palinurus, crosses the river Styx (which Palinurus, being unburied, may not pass), encounters Dido in the Mourning Fields, meets Deiphobus, a Trojan warrior, and passes into the light of Elysium, the place of the happy dead. He finds Anchises, who fortifies him by showing him the spirits who will be reincarnated as Rome's great men; there is lavish praise of Augustus. Aeneas notices a melancholy spirit: he will be Marcellus (Augustus' nephew) and will die young.

Book 7. The Trojans sail to the mouth of the Tiber. An omen indicates that the end of their troubles is nigh. They are welcomed by Latinus, king of Latium, who sees in Aeneas the fulfilment of an oracle that his daughter Lavinia shall wed a foreign husband. Juno, unable to thwart destiny, resolves nevertheless to cause the Trojans as much pain as she can. Her agent, the fury Allecto, arouses the passions of Amata, Lavinia's mother, and Turnus, prince of the Rutuli, who seeks Lavinia's hand. Ascanius kills a stag which, unknown to him, is a child's pet, and Allecto stirs up the anger of the local peasantry; there is a skirmish, and a few deaths. Preparations are made for war. A roll call of Italian warriors concludes the book.

Book 8. In a vision the river god Tiber welcomes Aeneas. Aeneas goes up river to Pallanteum, a settlement of Greeks. Evander, their king, gives him a guided tour of the place (which we know will become the site of Rome). Evander offers his support, and entrusts his son Pallas to Aeneas; he tells Aeneas that more effective support can be obtained from an alliance with the Etruscans. Venus appears to her son, bringing a shield depicting scenes from the future history of Rome; in its centre is Augustus defeating Cleopatra and Mark Antony at the Battle of Actium.

Books 9-11. War in Latium. Episodes include: the exploits of the Trojans Euryalus and his lover Nisus, who are killed through Euryalus' folly; Turnus' killing of Pallas; Aeneas' killing of the tyrant Mezentius and his admirable son Lausus; Evander's grief; a debate among the Trojans' adversaries between Drances, who wants to sue for peace, and Turnus, who wants to fight on; the exploits and death of the Italian warrior maiden Camilla.

Book 12. Turnus agrees to settle the issue of the war by single combat with Aeneas. Jupiter persuades Juno to accept the inevitable fulfilment of destiny. Aeneas has Turnus at his mercy; he thinks of sparing him, but then, seeing that he is wearing Pallas' sword-belt, angrily kills him.

Chapter 1

The Homeric Question

For two hundred years the study of Homer has been haunted by the 'Homeric question'. In simple terms, this is the question whether the *Iliad* and the *Odyssey* are each the work of one man or of many; and this is where any consideration of these poems has to begin. The Homeric question is not merely an antiquarian problem: an understanding of the issues can help us better to appreciate and enjoy the poems as works of art; and the easiest way to grasp the Homeric question itself is to look at how it has developed historically.

A very small number of the ancient Greeks thought that the poet of the *Odyssey* was a different man from the poet of the *Iliad*, but the vast majority supposed that both were by the same author, and no one seems to have doubted that each poem in itself was the work of a single mind. The Jewish historian Josephus suggested that Homer might have been illiterate; otherwise, the ancients appear to have assumed that he wrote his poems down. The first doubts about the unity of Homer were heard in the seventeenth century, but as a scholarly issue the Homeric question begins at the end of the eighteenth century with the German scholar F.A. Wolf, who argued for a multiplicity of authorship. After Wolf, those who took an interest in the question divided into two camps, later nicknamed 'unitarians' and 'analysts'. The unitarian position was simple: each poem was by a single man in the same straightforward sense that *Hamlet* is by Shakespeare. Analyst theories were of two main kinds. According to the first kind each poem accumulated gradually as one poet after another added his contribution. According to the second a 'redactor' or editor formed the poem by putting together a number of previously existing works, adding linking material of his own. In either case the picture is of a patchwork quilt. In the first case the quilt gets bigger as each poet stitches on his own piece; in the second the redactor himself stitches together a number of pieces made by other people.

Such were the competing theories until about sixty years ago, when the Homeric question was transformed by the American scholar Milman Parry. He made a detailed study of the repeated phrases in Homer, which he called formulae, and especially of those phrases which consist of a noun and an epithet ('wine-dark sea', 'Zeus the cloud gatherer', etc.). Here he found a kind of system, marked by what he called scope and economy. Scope meant that for each commonly occurring name or thing (battle, ships, wine) there was a formula available; economy meant that for each name or thing in each grammatical case there would be one formula only for a given amount of metrical space. Thus if the poet wants to fill two feet of metrical space with Achilles in the nominative case he calls him *dios Akhilleus*, 'godlike Achilles'; if he wants to fill two and a half feet he says *podas ōkus Akhilleus*, 'swift-footed Achilles', and so on. Parry concluded that the poet was not interested in Achilles' nobility in the one case or his fleetness in the other, but that metrical need was his only consideration.

Now Homer's Greek could never have been a spoken language. It contains a variety of dialect forms, which we know to come from different parts of the Greek world; and there is clear evidence in the grammar or scansion of some of the formulae which indicates that they were devised much earlier than the poems as we have them (to take an English comparison, if we find that a poem uses 'ye' for 'you' or rhymes 'obey' with 'tea', we expect it to have been written long before the late twentieth century). We believe also that Greece, which had writing in Mycenean times, went through some centuries of illiteracy before the eighth century BC. If we put together all the evidence the conclusion must be that some at least of the Homeric formulae must be older than the *Iliad* and *Odyssey* as we know them and have been transmitted orally, without the use of writing.

The idea that these epics were oral poetry – that is, the product of a non-literate society – was not new. We have seen that it goes back to Josephus, and it was revived in the eighteenth century by Robert Wood, an English amateur (who believed in a single Homer), and Wolf (who did not). Parry's contribution was to show that the whole technique of the poems was oral and passed from one bard to another: in the absence of writing, the bard was able to compose and perhaps improvise because he had learnt a large repertoire of pre-existing lines and phrases; obsolete forms and dialect variations were preserved because of their metrical usefulness. Parry demonstrated that the poems are in an oral *tradition*. He did not prove that Homer himself, if there was such a person, had no contact with writing, and scholars continue to argue whether our *Iliad* was composed wholly without the assistance of writing or whether it came into being at a time when an orally trained poet could get his work recorded, either by dictation or by learning to write himself. Parry's theory has needed to be modified in various ways – in particular, we now think that the Homeric poems use formulae more flexibly than he supposed – but essentially it holds good. Like Newtonian physics, it is a good working model for most purposes.

Parry's work does not do away with the Homeric question, but it makes it very different. (To make matters clearer, I shall now speak only of the *Iliad*.) The analyst now supposes that the *Iliad* is formed over generations as one bard after another sings the story of Troy and Achilles and passes it down to his successors. The analogy must now be not with a patchwork but with a rumour. Suppose I tell you a rumour. You tell it to your friend A, putting it in your own words; A tells it to B, muddling up the people involved; B adds some spicier details; C connects it up with another story he has heard. By the time the story gets back to me it is unrecognisable. But it makes little sense to ask 'Who composed this rumour?' It is re-composed each time it is told. Analysts can now depict the *Iliad* as coming into being rather like this. Of course one bard may have been particularly inventive, while another may have passed on what he heard with little change, but essentially the poem (on this account) is the collective work of a tradition.

The unitarian's position is changed too. 'Of course I accept', he now says, 'that Homer used phrases inherited from other bards, very likely whole lines, maybe whole paragraphs and story patterns; and as he reworked them, perhaps he refashioned them entirely, perhaps changed them little. But I still believe in a single genius who created the *Iliad* out of the raw materials provided by his tradition and to whom we can attribute the poem's greatness of scale and quality.' Some unitarians think that we have Homer's *Iliad* pretty much as he composed it; others that the poem was transmitted orally for a period after Homer and underwent change in the process. If the change was large, the boundaries between unitarianism and analysis start to become blurred: the conception of a 'monumental poem' which is then continuously altered by oral transmission is not totally different from the conception of a continuously evolving poem in which at least one individual played a specially creative part.

There is not space here to adjudicate between the rival theories, though the problem remains a fascinating intellectual challenge (in Britain at least most scholars are now unitarians of some sort). But one warning should be sounded. In recent years some scholars have become bored with the stress on 'orality' and have deliberately treated the Homeric poems just like any other literary masterpiece. That is fair enough and has produced some outstanding criticism. Behind some of this writing, though, there lurks an embarrassment with the oral basis of Homeric technique, a feeling that it will be to Homer's discredit if we cannot make him as sophisticated, as much like a poet of Virgil's type, as we can. In what follows I shall try to indicate that, on the contrary, the oral style has virtues peculiar to itself, that the primitive elements in Homer have a species of power and profundity denied to more sophisticated poetries, that we should enjoy and rejoice in the way that tradition and formulae are exploited to form a distinctive vision of the world.

But first, for clarity's sake, I shall confess my own opinions. Some people recoil from the thought that a great poem might be the work of many minds; they hope keenly that it may be possible to believe in a single Homer. I do not share that feeling, and find the idea of the *Iliad* as a collective work of the Greek imagination quite appealing, but for mainly technical reasons I think that it is unlikely to be right. I am therefore a modified unitarian. That is compatible with believing that there may have been interpolations into the poems since Homer sang; thus I share the widespread view that Book 10 of the *Iliad* is an addition by another poet. In parts of the *Odyssey* there are certain oddities and disorders which I think, tentatively, may be most easily explained on the supposition that it is, in some sense, an unfinished poem. Perhaps the poet sang his *Odyssey* or parts of it in various versions without resolving all his ideas and materials into a fully finished whole, and one or two places were patched by pupils. Most experts believe that the poet of the *Iliad* and the poet of the *Odyssey* cannot be the same man; I am not so sure. In what follows I shall try to bring out the differences between the two epics; but they are both special and artificial constructs, experiments in interpreting the world, and I think that both could be the product of one great creative imagination, bent on telling two different sorts of story and exploring different aspects of human experience. It may be that there are good grounds for deciding that the *Odyssey* cannot be by the poet of the *Iliad*, but if so, these are likely to be technical matters of language rather than differences in theology, morality or 'view of life'. I shall use the name of Homer when talking about both poems, but that is merely a convenient shorthand; if readers want to substitute 'the *Odyssey* poet', 'the poetic tradition' or whatever, they should not find that the argument is affected.

Chapter 2
Formulae and the Homeric View of Life

If we take Homer's repeated phrases and sentences seriously, we find that they create a particular kind of world: men are brave and godlike, women beautiful and chaste, the earth bountiful. It is a world in which the ordinary, simple actions and appetites of life are celebrated; so that the business of putting a mast in its socket and raising a sail or cutting up meat and roasting it on spits is worth describing in full.

And sure enough, the action of the *Iliad* fits this picture. Marriage is good and indissoluble; so much so, that the single adultery in the poem has caused the whole Trojan War. There is no rape, prostitution or homosexuality; nor in the *Odyssey* either. The *Iliad* is also an epic without villains, in this respect, strikingly unlike most heroic song. We might expect Paris to be the villain of the piece, but he is not. Though frivolous, he is rather an engaging character; his conciliatory response to Hector's rebuke (13. 775ff.) can be compared to Diomedes' admirably cool acceptance of Agamemnon's unjust reproaches in Book 3 and the prudent Antilochus' disarming reply to an angry Menelaus in Book 23. He is also an effective if inconstant warrior and it will be he who finally brings about Achilles' death.

The issue raised by formulaic language is brought out in a disagreement between the two most famous critics of the Victorian age, John Ruskin and Matthew Arnold. In the third book Helen looks from the walls for her two brothers, hoping to see them among the Achaean host. 'But the life-giving earth [*phusizoos aia*] already held them under, there in Lacedaemon, in their dear native land' (243f.) – in other words, they are dead. Ruskin gave this as an example of Homer's view of the world: the two are dead, but even so he will not speak of the earth in sadness or sorrow. Arnold retorted that Ruskin had failed to understand the nature of Homer's style – in our terms, he had not recognised that the language is formulaic. Now as it happens the phrase *phusizoos aia* comes nowhere else in the *Iliad*. That is itself significant; much more of the poem feels formulaic than really is so. We have every reason to believe that the pathetic contrast between the individual's death and the continuing vitality of nature as a whole was the poet's conscious design. But let us suppose that *phusizoos aia* were a recurrent phrase. The effect would be the same. It is the nature of the formulaic style, in the hands of a master, to produce such poignant dissonances.

The 'godlike' heroes are a case in point. An ancient critic said that Homer seemed to him to have made his men gods and his gods men. That was a shrewd remark; but the 'ungodlike' behaviour of Homer's deities, which so offended Plato, is not just light relief, it is at the heart of his idea of man. The heroes are indeed very like the gods, in all but two respects: men are mortal, whereas gods never die; gods are happy and men miserable. Again and again the formulae reassert these truths. To call the heroes godlike is at once a verity and a paradox: the heroes are so close to gods, and yet, facing the blank horror of death at any moment, so immensely far. That is part of the tragic vision.

This vision shines out of a famous simile:

> The generation of men is just like that of leaves. The wind scatters one year's leaves on the ground, but the forest burgeons and puts out others, as the season of spring comes round. So it is with men: one generation grows on, and another is passing away.
>
> (6. 146ff.)

This simile was to be imitated and developed by later Greek poets, and in due course by Virgil, from whom it passed on to Dante and Milton. Almost all these poets give it a melancholy inflexion, a dying fall: only Homer looks onward beyond autumn to the next spring and nature's everlasting power of strength and renewal. Compare the life-giving earth in the third book. In one sense the *Iliad* is an immensely high-spirited poem. Life, it declares, is full of vigour and energy; and life is everything, for there is nothing, or at least nothing worthy of our desire, after death. This is wonderful and yet terrible, since life can only be lived to the fullest at the risk of being cut brutally short. For the finest thing in life, the highest expression of human greatness, is war. Battle is glorious, *kudianeira* – once again the formula tells a mighty truth – but it is also cruel, miserable and humiliating. Therefore the hero's life is both immensely desirable and immensely wretched; it is a deeply tragic idea.

Homeric language has a peculiar transparency; it takes the colour of its context. A simple example can be found in the last book. When Priam decides to go to Achilles, his wife tries to dissuade him: how can he bear to go into the presence of the man who has killed so many of his sons – 'Your heart must be of iron' (202ff.). That is bitter reproach. When Achilles sees Priam, he repeats these lines, to very moving effect, for their force has been transmuted from anger to pity and admiration (519ff.). Yet the language, except for the necessary change of one unimportant word and the alteration of a single letter in another, remains exactly the same.

That is an unambiguous case; in others judgement may be more subjective. In the second book Homer describes the mobilisation of the Achaean army in terms that evoke the brilliance and splendour of military panoply.

> Then war became a sweeter thought to them than returning
> in their hollow ships to their own dear native land
> (2. 453f.)

Here we seem to celebrate the excitement of action. At the start of Book 11 the Achaeans deploy again: their circumstances are now sterner and the poet's tone darker. That sternness is the more keenly felt when the two lines from Book 2 are repeated (11. 13f.), for in the new context there now seems something grim in these men being so possessed by battle that they prefer it to the thought of home. That grimness would be less if the same words had not sounded before in a brighter key. Or so we may feel. Much of the *Iliad* works upon us in this way; hard and objective in its outward manner, it yet invites us to a personal and emotional response.

Thus the *Iliad*'s style helps to establish a certain attitude to life, a remarkable amalgam of sharp-edged realism and tender feeling; we find it in the battle scenes which make up the greater part of the work. It is said that the *Iliad* is from end to end about death. That sounds grand and noble; more exactly, most of the *Iliad* is about killing. Homer's picture of battle illustrates how artificiality and realism may enhance each other. In many respects his battles are formalised and unreal. No hero is killed by a common soldier or a stray arrow from the melée. No one is crippled or dies from his wounds; either death is immediate or a wound is superficial and soon healed. Aeschylus' account of the Trojan War, in his tragedy *Agamemnon*, tells us about lice and boredom; Homer ignores these realities of campaigning life. But by formalising or excluding so much he concentrates upon the fact of killing. The spear's passage through the body, or downwards, or across; bone smashed, guts spilled. To the layman it sounds anatomically precise, and some medical experts at least have agreed that it is. Homer's eye is not only objective but unblinking; he does not flinch. Yet it is not gruesome as Lucan is, and sometimes even Virgil. He is exact; neither lurid nor evasive. Homer saw death steadily and saw it whole.

Chapter 3
Characterisation in the Iliad

The portrayal of character is one of the first things that most people look for when they read a novel or see a play, and it is natural to ask how far this may be found in Homer. Discussion of this topic is sometimes rather muddled, and it will be as well to consider at the outset just what 'characterisation' means. Commonly people use the term to cover two different things, which I shall call individuation and psychological penetration. Let me offer an analogy to explain this.

Most of Dickens' characters are very clearly individuated. Micawber, Pecksniff, Uriah Heep, Mrs Gamp, all have their distinctive attitudes, mannerisms and modes of behaviour; so much so that we could recognise them if we met them in the street or pick them out at an identity parade. But it has been said that they have no insides; you cannot imagine what it would be like to be Heep or Micawber. And commonly they are without variation: Pecksniff is always a hypocrite, Chadband always sanctimonious. But two of Dickens' novels are told entirely in the first person – David Copperfield narrates the book that bears his name and Pip narrates *Great Expectations* – and here the technique is different. David and Pip do not have a great deal of individuation – they have some but nothing like as much as Dickens' comic grotesques: you would not recognise them if you met them. But through their narrations we have a marvellous insight into how it feels to be a boy or a young man; how, for example, a child's mind experiences grief or fear or thwarted pride. That is psychological penetration.

Of course it is possible for an author so to portray a character that individuation and psychological penetration are both present. But the important point to grasp is that these things are in principle different. When critics refer to characterisation they usually seem to mean individuation, but sometimes they confuse this with psychological insights that are not necessarily individuated at all. Bearing this in mind, let us see what kinds of characterisation we can find in the *Iliad*.

Achilles is strongly individuated. Homer's first line tells us the subject of his poem: not the Trojan War, not even Achilles, but

Achilles' behaviour. 'Sing, goddess, of the anger of Achilleus, son of Peleus'; in the Greek *mēnis*, wrath or anger, is the very first word of all. And as the story unfolds, it becomes clear that his behaviour is unique; even Patroclus cannot understand it. The *Iliad* differs from other heroic poems in that the individual nature of the protagonist makes the plot. That is not true of the *Odyssey* or *Aeneid*; of course Aeneas and Odysseus need great virtues to overcome their troubles, but those troubles are visited upon them by forces outside themselves. But if Achilles had been like Diomedes there would not be an *Iliad* at all and if he had been like Agamemnon it would have ended at Book 9.

The Homeric hero's ideal is to be 'a speaker of words and a doer of deeds' – that is the aim Achilles' father urged upon him (9. 443). This is a striking conception of prowess, honouring sharpness of mind alongside strength of arm, and it was to be of immense importance for later epics in the classical tradition: Odysseus, Aeneas, Adam are all people whose mental lives are of absorbing interest. How different Siegfried in the *Nibelungenlied* or the warlords of *Njal's Saga*. The epithet *kudianeira*, glorious, is applied to the assembly (*agorē*) as well as to battle, formulaic language once more shaping a certain perception of the world: both are fields of competitive endeavour in which human excellence may be displayed. Achilles is supposed to be a fine orator, though not the finest: he himself says that whereas he is the greatest of warriors others surpass him in debate (18. 105f.). The unfolding of the poem suggests that he is too modest: he has the *Iliad*'s greatest speeches.

Not only is Achilles the most intellectual of Homer's warriors; he is the only artist among them. In Book 9 we see him singing the deeds of men, accompanying himself on the lyre (186, 189). In the *Odyssey* minstrels are performers in aristocratic households, honoured but subordinate – a position which doubtless reflects the reality of the world in which Homer sang. To make the greatest man of action into the only poet in the story is a bold and striking idea. The only other artist in the *Iliad* is Helen, who is first seen embroidering a tapestry which depicts the Trojan War itself (3. 125ff.). Later she looks to the future and sees Paris and herself becoming a subject of song for men yet to come (6. 357f.). In reality and in imagination she transmutes her experiences into art. In a strange way Helen is more like Achilles than anyone else in the *Iliad*; both are reflective, combining intense emotion with a curious detachment by means of which they can see themselves through other people's eyes. Each has a divine parent, and each is encompassed by a certain strangeness.

The poetic and reflective side of Achilles is not merely something that we are told about and asked to take on trust; we hear it for ourselves in his utterances. The *Iliad* is full of similes; the vast majority of them come in the battle scenes, very few in speeches. Achilles, though, does use similes. In Book 9 he likens his deeds in battle, fighting for a cause that is not his own, to a mother bird who brings morsels to her chicks, faring badly herself (323f.). Though he speaks with passionate anger, the comparison is quaint, unexpected, almost one may say amusing. Later, when Patroclus comes to him weeping, he will liken him to a little girl who runs along beside her mother, tugging at her dress, holding her back, crying until mother picks her up (16. 7ff.). The simile is odd, teasing, affectionate, ironically self-aware in its perception that Patroclus will get what he wants out of his friend. If we try to imagine Agamemnon, Odysseus, even Hector talking like that, we shall realise how finely the simile characterises Achilles himself. He is the wittiest man in the *Iliad*. The simile also forms part of a pattern of imagery: in Book 23 the poet himself will liken Achilles to a parent, a father lamenting over the ashes of his son. That comparison is poignantly ironic, because Achilles is mourning a man older than himself, but it gains force also from its relation to Achilles' own idea of himself in a 'parental' role.

Agamemnon too is well characterised. As we shall see, the difference between his way of talking and Achilles' will become part of the poem's moral economy. Some accounts of the *Iliad* present him as merely irresolute and mean-spirited; that is at best an incomplete picture, for he is also a lord of men and a great warrior. It is not only the formulae that tell us this: he has the longest arming scene in the poem and an impressive *aristeia* (scene of prowess). There is a counterpoint between formalism and naturalism in the *Iliad*, between the grand and the ordinary, and if we see Agamemnon only in everyday terms, as though he came out of a realistic novel of modern life, we shall miss half of what Homer is telling us.

The poet may choose to individuate a quite minor character. Antilochus, for example, only springs into prominence in Book 23, during the funeral games for Patroclus, where he is vividly depicted as a young man of cool head and steady nerves, who gets what he wants by shrewd flexibility. Before the chariot race he listens to his father's advice to overtake at the turning post, says nothing, but overtakes at a different place. He gets past Menelaus by calculating that Menelaus' nerve will break first; which it does. At the distribution of prizes, when Menelaus protests, Antilochus completely outwits him by deferring so gracefully that Menelaus finds himself yielding up the prize that Antilochus had wanted all along; it is perhaps the funniest moment in the poem. When he speaks to Achilles, by contrast, he stands up fiercely for his rights, reckoning (we may infer) that self-assertion will appeal to the proudest of the Achaeans; and so it does. This sparkling characterisation is fitting not because Antilochus is central to the *Iliad* but because during the games this tragic poem turns briefly into a comedy of manners. This is not only, or even primarily, because the poet wants a light interlude between two episodes of high emotion. Books 23 and 24 both study the ending of Achilles' wrath and his recovery of sympathy with others, the former by showing him in relation to his society, the latter by showing him face to face with a single man. Social comedy is appropriate to the games because they are the revelation of the social Achilles. When Antilochus makes his protest, Achilles smiles (555). It is a great moment: for twenty-two and a half books Achilles has had nothing to smile about; suddenly he feels a spontaneous pleasure. We believe in that smile because we have met Achilles and Antilochus as individuals, and we understand why Antilochus should be Achilles' 'dear friend' (556). We are amused and delighted by him, and Achilles joins in our pleasure.

This suggests that individuation is one of the tricks in Homer's bag; it may suit him to individuate quite a minor character, and conversely a major character may be colourless. I cannot see any individuality in Sarpedon at all, and little even in Hector. True, he is over-confident, neglecting Polydamas' warnings, but even this seems to be more the common character of man, ignorant as he is of the future, than a strongly personal trait. Hector is contrasted with Achilles in various ways: Achilles is at Troy for glory, Hector to defend his city; Achilles is isolated, whereas Hector is embedded in a setting, seen in relation to parents, wife, child, brothers, city. But these are differences of situation, not of character; indeed one of the differences between the two men is that Achilles is keenly individuated, Hector not. This is not a fault in the poem but a strength, enabling Homer to study humanity by a variety of means. In one sense Hector is a wholly exceptional man, a great warrior, one who can pick up a stone that two men today could hardly lift; but in another he is every man, an ordinary person with ordinary experiences. None of us is an Achilles; each of us may be, in some degree, a Hector. Through Hector's soliloquy in Book 22, Homer studies how a man steels himself to a course of action that he fears and hates; it is telling because we realise that it is true to common experience. We can share Hector's feelings (it would be an impertinence to attempt that with Achilles); he provides us with the emotion of recognition which Henry James set against the emotion of surprise as one of literature's legitimate pleasures.

Characterisation in the *Iliad* seems to owe much to the tradition. Commonly the most individuated people tend to be those about whom we know myths independent of Homer: Agamemnon, Ajax, Odysseus, Paris. Odysseus is shrewd in the *Iliad*, Paris inconstant, because they were shrewd and inconstant long before Homer sang. Conversely, the colourless figures seem to have been invented, or at least largely developed, for the *Iliad* itself. But this should not disturb us; it is Homer's pleasure to work with the grain of a tradition.

Even where there is individuation, it is not necessarily to be understood in terms of realistic characterisation. Take Helen. Unlike Paris, she seems strangely cocooned from blame (though she blames herself). When she goes out on to the walls, the old men remark that it is no wonder that the Trojans have been willing to suffer so much for her sake, as 'she is fearfully like the immortal goddesses to look at' (3. 156ff.). Outside Homer, we find a story apparently designed to protect her. The lyric poet Stesichorus was said to have been sent blind for insulting her; he wrote a recantation saying that it was only her phantom which went to Troy: the real Helen was on a ten-year holiday in Egypt. She was the daughter of Leda, who had been doubly impregnated, by her husband Tyndareus and by the god Zeus, consequently bearing two pairs of twins, one pair being male (Castor and Polydeuces), one female (Helen and Clytemnestra). Polydeuces was immortal, Castor mortal; and one of the female pair should be immortal, by the same token. Clytemnestra was undoubtedly mortal; which leaves Helen. And sure enough, we find that she was worshipped as a goddess at Sparta. It looks as though she is a goddess who has somehow got into the Troy story. She is fearfully like the goddesses to look at – well, yes indeed. Now let there be no mistake: in the *Iliad* she is wholly mortal; but traces of a different myth survive. Once more, this is not a fault in the poem: the vestiges of a lost idea give Helen her mysterious, indefinable charm. Such suggestive playing with the tradition is more typical of the *Odyssey* than the *Iliad*, but indeed the *Iliad*'s Helen is presented with a softness, a blurriness more Odyssean than its predominantly hard and masculine tone. In the *Odyssey* itself she is mysterious: she has learnt of magic drugs which take away care, and we learn that when the wooden horse was brought into Troy, she walked round it imitating the voices of the wives of the men inside (4. 277ff.). Why? And how did she know what they sounded like? There are no answers to such questions, and it is misguided to look for a realistic explanation for her behaviour (women are such devious creatures, or whatever). Instead, the story has the illogicality and inconsequentiality of a folktale. In the *Iliad* too it is prosaic to explain her individuality in terms of naturalistic characterisation: we lose the charms of impalpability.

Chapter 4
Heroism and Tragedy

The colourlessness of Sarpedon, like the near colourlessness of
Hector, enables the poet to deepen his tragic idea in a way that would
not be possible otherwise. Homer establishes a parallelism between
these two men. In Book 12, as the Trojans advance, each is given a
simile comparing him to a lion which is brave and aggressive but killed
or wounded through its very courage (41ff., 299ff.). Theirs are the two
most important deaths on the Trojan side in the poem, and as we shall
see, each is preceded by a very similar scene between gods. When we
first meet Sarpedon, in Book 5, it is to Hector that he is speaking,
reproaching him for the Trojans' feebleness in the fight:

> But we are fighting, we allies in your city. I am one of them,
> an ally come from a great distance. Lycia is far away, by the
> swirling river Xanthus, and there I have left behind my dear
> wife and my infant son, and much property, the envy of
> every poor man. And yet for all that I spur on my Lycians
> and am eager myself to face my man in battle – but I have
> nothing here that the Achaeans might loot or carry off. But
> you just stand there idle, and do not even give orders to the
> rest of your people to hold their ground and fight in defence
> of their wives.
>
> (477ff.)

So Sarpedon has a wife and one baby son – in this just like Hector.
But though he is on the Trojans' side, he does not fight for kin or city;
he just fights. He risks the good things he has, and for no obvious
purpose; like the Achaean chiefs he is there simply to act as a hero
should. We are interested in him not as a distinctive individual, but
for the role that he has to play.

Fitly, then, it is he who expresses the essence of the heroic idea
in its purest form, and fitly it is to his fellow Lycian Glaucus that he
expresses it. They two, he says, are held in highest honour by the
Lycians; they have the richest farmland, get the best of the meat and
the wine, and 'all look on us like gods'. Therefore they should face the
battle,

so that among the heavy-armoured Lycians people will say:
'These are no worthless men who rule over us in Lycia,
these kings we have who eat our fat sheep and drink the
choice of our honey-sweet wine. No, they have strength too
and courage, since they fight at the front of the Lycian
lines.'

(12. 310ff.)

Sarpedon is not talking about a kind of social contract (the Lycians
give us privileges and in return it is our duty to protect them): Glaucus
and he must fight not for the sake of the Lycians but in order that the
Lycians may praise them. Indeed, he cannot be talking about a social
contract, for hear how he continues: 'Dear friend, if we were going to
live for ever, ageless and immortal, if we survived this war, then I
would not be fighting in the front ranks myself or urging you into
glorious battle [*makhēn es kudianeiran*].' If they were carrying out a
duty towards the Lycians, immortality would enable them to fulfil it
all the better. The tragic paradox is that the hero's role is worthwhile
only because it is useless and because its splendour is always an inch
away from the misery and ugliness of death.

At some periods people admire the primitive in art and liter-
ature, at others they disdain it. At present there seems to be a
revulsion against primitivism, and some scholars try to make Homer's
morality as advanced and modern as they can. They hope to find in
his heroes a concern not only for their own honour and glory but also
for the 'cooperative' virtues on which our own society places more
value, such as duty and loyalty. To claim that Sarpedon is talking about
his duty or loyalty to the Lycians is to go flat against the words that
Homer has given him; but notice, in any case, that the tragic profund-
ity of Homer's idea lies in the very absence of such more 'advanced'
values in this place. Battle is *kudianeira*, and a hero must fight as the
expression of his greatness; but this is not – or at least not in an
ordinary sense – a selfish intent. Sarpedon does not want to fight – if
he were lucky enough to be a god, he would not do so – and as we
have seen he has a wife and child and wealth, all of which he may lose,
and for ever. And it is all futile: the Lycians are not threatened, and
gain nothing by it; Sarpedon's family risk only wretchedness. There
lies the tragedy: if Sarpedon could say with Horace, 'Dulce et deco-
rum est pro patria mori', if he could speak of duty to others and see
his death as a service to his fellow men, there would be a softening of
the hard facts, and some consolation. But he cannot; the *Iliad* is not
in the business of consolation.

The same 'primitivism' makes the terror of Hector's death. He dreads facing Achilles; why then does he go? It is not for the sake of others: Priam tells him that if he goes, he will be killed, and his death will lead on to the fall of Troy and the slaughter of Priam himself (22. 38ff.); and we know this to be true. Hector's reason is this:

> I feel shame [*aideomai*] before the men of Troy and the women of Troy with their trailing dresses, that some man, a worse man than I, will say: 'Hector trusted in his own strength and destroyed his people'.
>
> (22. 105ff.)

Fig. 1. Achilles and Hector fight (from a mixing-bowl, about 490 BC). This scene, slightly different from the Iliad's account, catches its spirit: man confronts man, face to face; the gods, both involved and detached, give significance to the action. Athena guides Achilles (she 'will beat you down under my spear', he tells Hector, 22. 270f.); Apollo abandons Hector (231) but with a gesture indicating that he will bring about Achilles' own death (359f.).

As with Sarpedon and the Lycians, it is a question of what his people will say, not what is in their interest: the great man must act, at whatever cost to himself or others, to maintain his greatness; therein lies the splendour of humanity. Hector is not in the ordinary sense standing on his dignity. On the contrary, the cruel paradox is that his action will lead to his humiliation: the Achaeans will taunt and disfigure his freshly dead body, and Achilles will drag his unburied corpse around the walls of Troy. The tragedy is that Hector's sacrifice is useless to himself; more terrible still, it is worse than useless to the Trojans also, since, as Priam says, it will hasten Troy's end. Such is the cost of heroism.

Before Patroclus kills Sarpedon, there is a scene among the gods (16. 431ff.). Zeus, Sarpedon's father, wonders if he should save his son. Hera, the wife of Zeus, intervenes, tersely urging him not to rescue a man already marked for death: 'Do it then – but we other gods will not all approve you.' She adds a consolation: let the gods Sleep and Death honour Sarpedon by carrying his body back to Lycia. Zeus concedes at once: it is not worth his while to disturb the concord of the gods. He rains tears of blood to honour his dear son, but he does not seem greatly affected (when the god Ares lost a son in Book 14, his upset was even more brief and superficial).

The oral style, with its habit of repetition, achieves a powerfully tragic effect when this scene is 'replayed' before Hector's death (22. 167ff.). Again Zeus considers whether to save a man dear to him; and the second time round his words are chilling. We know now that he has not troubled to rescue even his own son; how much more hopeless is Hector's position, for all the apparent benevolence in Zeus' words. Once more a goddess, this time Athena, warns him off, but on this occasion there is no consolation added. Zeus' reply is extraordinary: Do not worry, he tells her, I was not speaking seriously. The tone is casual, almost flippant; but there is terror for man in the divine lightness.

How then do the gods regard mankind? On the one hand they seem to be passionately involved in the Trojan War (two of them are even wounded there, and two lose their sons); on the other, the formulae tell us that they are happy and free from care, and much of the action bears this out. In Book 22, as Achilles chases Hector, the two men are compared to horses racing; they run swiftly, though

> it was no sacrificial beast or oxhide shield they were competing for – such as are the usual prizes that men win

in the foot-race – but they were running for the life of
Hector tamer of horses.

(158ff.)

Meanwhile all the gods look on. The sporting analogy still speaks to
us directly: when we watch the big match, on one level we are
passionately anxious that Spurs should beat West Ham, or whatever,
while on another it does not matter to us at all. We leave the stadium,
and our lives are unchanged. The gods are like that. It would be wrong
to apply to them the words which Shakespeare gives Gloucester in
King Lear: 'As flies to wanton boys, so are we to the gods: They kill us
for their sport.' Homer's gods are not cosmic sadists; their essence is
rather in the lightness of their emotions. On one level they are keenly
caught up in the great game of the war, but deep down they do not
care a whit. Their nature is to be free from care, as Achilles tells Priam
in Book 24, and as the *Odyssey* will repeat (6. 42ff.), even though that
poem draws a more 'moral' picture of the gods. The Christian idea is
that God is great because he loves us. Homer's idea is the reverse of
this: the gods' greatness resides in the very fact that they do not need
to feel for us at all. And so their frivolity does not diminish them; it is
the touchstone of their divinity.

Chapter 5
The Wrath of Achilles

Achilles' behaviour raises acutely the question of how far we need to depart from our modern morality to understand the poem. There is a view of the *Iliad* which sees it as a moral drama pivoting on the ninth book; it goes something like this. Achilles may not behave perfectly in Book 1, but essentially he is justified in what he does, and Agamemnon is not. But Achilles goes disastrously astray in Book 9, when through anger he rejects a fair offer of restitution. His folly leads to the death of Patroclus, which leads him into more cruelty and wrong, until he magnificently recovers himself in the last two books.

That is quite an impressive picture of effect following upon cause, of a great man wounded by a tragic fault. And perhaps the largeness of the *Iliad* is such that it allows this as one way of understanding it. But the poem tells us that this is not the best or deepest way. Many people are glad to find flaws in Achilles and the other heroes; students write essays in which they say that characters with faults are 'more human' – as though Mother Teresa were less human than you and I. The truth is rather that very good or very great people are much harder to depict; if an author can bring such a portrait off, he will have achieved one of the rarest feats in literature. But let us look closer at Book 9.

The first thing to note is that when the ambassadors come to Achilles, he is courteous and welcoming. He is not 'sulking in his tent', as the proverb has it; his 'wrath' is not a fit of temper but a matter of settled, reasoned policy. The outburst of magnificent rage with which he responds to the news of Agamemnon's offer comes as a bolt from the blue; the poet has designed it to be a surprise, and our own response should be to ask what has inspired it.

The gifts that Agamemnon offers are of enormous value; Homer has deliberately made them so in order that there may be no question of Achilles rejecting the recompense because it is not big enough. The cause of the rejection must lie elsewhere. When Agamemnon gives the ambassadors their instructions, he tells Odysseus what to say, ending with these words: 'Let him yield...and let him submit to me, in that I am the greater king [*basileuteros*] and can claim to be his senior in age' (9. 158ff.). In accordance with the oral-formulaic style, Odysseus repeats to Achilles Agamemnon's speech as near verbatim as possible; tactfully, though, he omits those last imprudent lines. But by a stroke of genius Homer has Achilles answer as though he had heard the offending words: he refuses the chance to marry one of Agamemnon's daughters – this had been part of the offer – declaring, 'Let him choose some other of the Achaeans, a man like himself, a higher king [*basileuteros*] than I' (391f.).

Achilles was advised by his father 'always to be bravest and best and excel over others' (11. 784). That is a competitive ideal: it is the hero's first and highest task to assert his own honour and greatness. That is what Achilles is doing here. On one level Agamemnon has lost the struggle completely and has agreed to pay massively for his folly; but on another level, as his own words have revealed, he is still asking Achilles to yield and submit. And Achilles' keenness of mind is such that he recognises this, even though Odysseus has suppressed the damaging words. Other heroes – Ajax, for example, and even Achilles' closest friend Patroclus – cannot understand why he turns Agamemnon down, but that is not because they are better men but because they are unaware of something that Achilles has rightly seen. He stands alone, and it would be comforting to say that this is because he is petulant; we should then have the easy, conventional moral that a bad temper gets you into trouble. That is the moral which some of the characters in the drama seem to draw, and part of Homer's greatness is to tempt us to that response, while he ponders a deeper and darker truth. It is the very greatness of Achilles – the sharpness of his mind, the purity of his heroism – that makes him act as he does.

Ajax is the last of the ambassadors to speak, and the briefest. He says that Achilles is pitiless and implacable, and asks him to think of his friends with kindness. It is tempting to think that Ajax has got to the heart of the matter: Achilles should be asked to think of others, whose lives are at risk. That is indeed the view which some scholars take; and Achilles can only answer, they add, that Ajax is really right but he is himself too angry to do the proper thing.

On further reflection, though, this interpretation ought to seem very implausible. We have seen how sharp Achilles' perceptions are; conversely, we should see that Ajax's are blunt. He is bewildered, and admits it: 'But the heart the gods have put in your breast is implacable and perverse, all because of a girl, one girl – but now we are offering you seven, the very finest, and much more besides' (636ff.). But it cannot be 'a girl, one girl' that is making Achilles act as he does: Agamemnon has offered to restore Briseis, and if Achilles wants her back, that is a further reason to accept. Ajax is out of his depth: brilliantly, Homer offers us the commonsense view, only to show us that it is inadequate to the complexity of the situation.

It would be surprising if stalwart, baffled Ajax were the man to reduce Achilles to embarrassed evasion, and indeed he does not: Achilles' reply is deeper and stranger than many critics realise. He tells Ajax that his feelings are divided – but in what sense? Ovid makes his Medea say, 'I see the better course and approve it; I follow the worse' (*Metamorphoses* 7. 20f.). St Paul says, 'The good that I would I do not: but the evil which I would not, that I do' (Romans 7. 19). In either case the mental conflict is one of reason against passion, moral duty against desire. It is easy to suppose that Achilles is saying the same thing – many people have thought so – but he is not. Let us examine the exact words:

> All that you have said seems much after my own feeling [*thumos*]. But my heart [*kradiē*] swells with anger [*kholos*] whenever I think of that time, how the son of Atreus treated me with contempt...'
>
> (645ff.)

Achilles does not say that Ajax is right after all; he does not say that reason pulls him in one direction and emotion in the other; instead, with a marvellous and terrible objectivity in the midst of his wrath, he looks into himself and he sees two emotions. He feels attracted to what Ajax says but he also feels anger towards Agamemnon, and the anger is the stronger emotion. That is the stark reality. *We* may feel that if a man says that he is angry, he is talking about something which he can and should control; but to impose that idea upon this poem is to ignore Homer's otherness. A great hero is entitled to his wrath and it imputes to him no blame – that is implied in the story of Meleager's wrath which Phoenix has just told (9. 523ff.) – but in any case Achilles sees his anger not as something he can cancel but as a hard fact that simply exists.

'Ah, but', some critics say, 'Achilles may not actually tell Ajax that he is in the right, but that is what he really means.' This is what we might call the paraphrastic fallacy, common enough in the criticism of classical literature but perhaps especially so in the study of Homer, thanks to a lingering and subconscious feeling that the poor old bard, lumbered with a crude oral technique, could not always manage to say what he wanted. A rough paraphrase will be good enough for Homer, and it may even give us his meaning better than he could himself. Such an attitude is as wrong as it is patronising to the poet; in fact, as we shall see, Achilles' way of confronting the great issues is coherent, consistent, and distinguished from that of Agamemnon.

We should notice that Achilles suffers for his decision from the start, even before he lets Patroclus go into battle. We are suddenly told in Book 9 that Achilles has a choice: between immortal glory at the price of death at Troy and a long life without glory but spent in his dear native land (410ff.). Evidently the poet has invented this choice, unmentioned in Book 1, because it is newly significant at this point – why? The answer must be that in this book Achilles gets trapped in a position which gives him the advantage of neither choice. He realises that he must abandon his threat to go home; such a retreat would be alien to his nature. But by affirming that he will not enter the battle he deprives himself of glory also. Homer traps Achilles in this miserable situation because he wants him to have our sympathy.

Fig. 2. Achilles mourns the loss of Briseis (from a cup of about 480 BC). Two heralds take the girl away; Achilles laments, wrapped in his clothing. His wrath is seen as grief, not as a fit of temper; his helmet, sword and spear can be glimpsed hanging in his tent, reminders that he is deprived not only of his woman but of the hope of glory also.

Let us notice too that his anger is not of that ugly kind that makes itself deaf to all appeal. When people sulk or lose their temper they do not listen to what others say to them, but Achilles is not like that. He has taken in what Ajax said, as we have seen: it is much after his own feeling. And he has surely listened to the other two ambassadors as well. Phoenix has told how Meleager ended his wrath and entered battle at the moment when the enemy were climbing the walls and trying to fire the city, and this inspires Achilles to say that he will not turn to the fight again until Hector is firing the ships. It was Odysseus who stressed the danger to the ships; Achilles has heard him also. When Patroclus pleads to be allowed into the battle, Achilles will yield to persuasion once more; he cannot go in Patroclus' place, however, because he must hold to his word spoken in Book 9:

> It seems I cannot after all be angry in my heart for ever –
> and yet I said I would put aside my anger only when the
> clamour of battle reached my own ships, no sooner.
> (16. 60ff.; Hammond's translation, slightly altered.)

It is a tragic irony that if only Achilles had been more thoroughly stubborn – as readers sometimes think he is – Patroclus need not have perished in the way he did. The combination of Achilles' assertive individualism – the heroic ideal – with some willingness to respond to the ambassadors is what undoes him.

The German philosopher Hegel held the essence of tragedy to be a clash of irreconcilables. He was led to this theory by Sophocles' *Antigone*. Creon, the king of Thebes, must uphold the civil order and rightly demands that the traitor Polyneices shall not be buried. Antigone, Polyneices' sister, upholds the divine order which requires one to bury one's kin, and disobeys Creon, at the cost of her own life. Antigone and Creon are both right and the clash between two competing rights, bringing with it the inevitability of suffering, is what makes the situation inherently tragic – or so Hegel said. This is surely a wrong account of *Antigone*, and it is probably not a true account of tragedy in general, but it can be claimed that the *Iliad* is tragic in just this way. The heroic imperative which leads Achilles to reject Agamemnon's offer clashes irreconcilably with the humane imperative which would bring him back into battle to help the Achaeans. The clash is irresoluble, and it can only bring disaster upon Patroclus and Achilles himself. The tragedy is in the starkness, the hopelessness of those facts. We should have some consolation if we could say that disaster would have been avoided if only the man had behaved a little better. But that moral cosiness is sternly denied us: the terrible truth is that Achilles' refusal is not a regrettable aberration, not a great man's momentary littleness, but a supreme expression of human magnificence.

The same tragic spirit is to be found later in Achilles' story. When the quarrel is patched up in Book 19, Agamemnon makes a long and rather rambling speech, which is much concerned with the question of responsibility. Near the start of it he says:

> The Achaeans before this have often said the same to me
> as you say now, and criticised me for it. But I am not to
> blame, but rather Zeus and Fate and Erinys that walks in
> darkness: they put a cruel blindness in my mind...
>
> (85ff.)

and he wanders off into a long story about the gods. Finally he gets back to the point: 'But since I was blinded and Zeus took away my wits...' It is a vivid portrayal of a man who needs to apologise but cannot do so gracefully. First he says the thing is not his fault; then he veers away from the subject, as though reluctant to look at it squarely; at last he seems momentarily to face the fact of his responsibility (the word translated as 'I was blinded' could be rendered as 'I went astray'), but at once he is trying to shuffle it off again ('and Zeus took away...'). Homer's psychology is very nice.

Learned men have gone astray here through trying to extract from this speech a Homeric view of causation and human responsibility. The question of how the early Greeks saw human action, divine action and the relation between them is a very interesting one, and the *Iliad* is one of the most important pieces of evidence we have, but we must not confuse trying to understand this issue with trying to understand the poem itself. Agamemnon is not a person with crystalline clarity of thought but a fallible man in an awkward situation; and unless we see his speech in its dramatic setting, we shall miss its effect. If someone says, 'Zeus did such-and-such to so-and-so', it is not necessarily either an excuse or a condemnation; it depends who is speaking and in what context. When Achilles says in Book 9 that Zeus the counsellor has robbed Agamemnon's wits (377), it is meant as an insult; when Agamemnon says the same of himself in Book 19, it is meant as exculpation. What Agamemnon's language does show clearly is that Homer's characters can talk in terms of responsibility and being at fault: 'I am not to blame' – the words could hardly be plainer.

Now let us turn back to Book 18 and see how Achilles reacts to Patroclus' death. We might expect him to say that it was his fault (or perhaps that it was not his fault), but he simply does not think in these terms at all; the contrast between his way of thinking and Agamemnon's is one of Homer's masterstrokes of construction and shows the range and profundity of his moral imagination. *ton apōlesa*, 'I have lost him,' Achilles says in the course of his first speech to his mother (82), and the words are heartbreaking, so bare, so brief; the plain stark fact set down with absolute simplicity, without elaboration or adornment. Achilles' second speech to Thetis is where people have most inclined to see him expressing guilt or remorse. Again, let us look at the exact words:

> Then let me die directly, since I was not to help my friend
> at his killing – he has died far away from his native land,
> and did not have me there to protect him from destruction.
> So now, since I shall not return to my dear native land, since
> I have not been a saving light to Patroclus or my many other
> companions...but sit here by the ships, a useless burden on
> the earth...oh, that quarrels should vanish from gods and
> men, and resentment [*kholos*], which drives even a man of
> good sense to anger! It is far sweeter to men than trickling
> honey, and swells to fill their hearts like smoke – such is the
> anger that Agamemnon, lord of men, has caused me now.
> (18. 98ff.)

If we listen to this attentively, we shall realise that there is no self-reproach here. With the terrible clarity that is his hallmark, Achilles sees the facts as they are, in all their tragic simplicity. 'I was not to help...', 'I have not been a light to Patroclus'; if only anger did not exist (not 'I was wrong to be angry', or 'I went astray'); Agamemnon has 'caused anger in me' (Achilles uses the verb *kholoo*, to make angry, from *kholos*). Friends of the paraphrastic fallacy maintain that Homer had no words to express ideas of guilt and responsibility, so that although Achilles does not actually say that he feels remorse, his words amount to the same thing. This attitude does little honour to Homer, but it is in any case plainly wrong, as we have seen from Agamemnon's speech in the next book. It is indeed Homer's genius to place these two different ways of seeing – Achilles' and Agamemnon's – in proximity. The poet shows us that Achilles could have spoken in very different terms; and the whole shape and progress of the poem enforces the feeling not that Achilles' vision is inferior to his fellows' but that it possesses a fearful verity.

When he returns to the battle, his killings are not inspired by guilt or remorse, nor by blood-lust, in any ordinary sense. Rage blinds the reason, but Achilles, in the midst of his passion, remains in a strange and fearsome way reasonable; his intellectual control does not slacken. His reply to Lycaon, who begs for his life to be spared, has been much admired for its terrifying cold clarity:

> Die, my friend, you too, for no one can escape death: why
> complain, since Patroclus, a better man than you, has died?
> – I am great and handsome, the son of a goddess, but the
> time is coming when I too shall be killed.
>
> (21. 106ff.)

This pitiless speech – and 'pitiless', *ameiliktos*, is Homer's own word – is almost gentle, intimate even, in the manner of its utterance. You, me, the dead – the bare lucidity with which Achilles sees each of these, and their relation one to another looks forward to the still bleaker truths which he will unfold to Priam. He understands, and he accepts; in this he is contrasted with Hector. As Patroclus is about to be killed he warns Hector that Achilles will avenge his slaughter; Hector's reply is insouciant: Why prophesy death for me? who knows if Achilles may not perish by my spear? (16. 859ff.) By a magnificent irony, Hector in his turn, the man who does not see the future, the natural man, is given a supernatural power of second sight at the moment of his own death: with perfect accuracy he prophesies to Achilles that Apollo and Paris will kill him by the Scaean gates (22. 359f.). Achilles does not dissent: 'Die; as for me, I shall receive my fate when Zeus and the other gods choose' (22. 365ff.). He knows where he stands in relation to the gods. He is the proudest man in the *Iliad*; perhaps he is also the most humble.

What he will not accept is that he can no longer do anything for Patroclus: he kicks against the limits of the human condition, the finality of death. The voice of dour realism is heard from Odysseus in Book 19; Achilles wants to fast, now that Patroclus is dead, but Odysseus urges him to have a meal before going into battle. Starving the belly is no way to mourn a dead man, he says (225ff.): too many men die on the battlefield in endless succession and we must harden our hearts, giving them the tears only of a day – then it is back to the grim business of killing. Gods see things differently from men, but a similar note is heard from Apollo in Book 24:

> I suppose before now a man has lost one yet more dear to
> him – a brother from the same womb, or a son: yet he weeps
> and laments and then is done, since the Fates have put an
> enduring heart in humankind.
>
> (46ff.)

Yet Achilles is still trying to injure Hector, though he is now nothing
but 'dumb earth'. Men's 'enduring heart' – the crude fact that they
have to put up with things, without too much fuss – is in contrast to
the behaviour of the gods. Just before Apollo speaks, the poet
mentions the judgement of Paris, for the only time in the poem: in
naming Aphrodite as the most beautiful of three goddesses, Paris had
dishonoured the other two, Hera and Athena, and they have
accordingly persisted in their hatred for Troy, and will persist until it
is utterly destroyed. A man 'laments and then is done', but a god may
maintain his grudge to the bitter end.

'Godlike Achilles' will find how immensely unlike a god he is in
this respect. In the later books his ruling motive seems to be the desire
to do something for his dead friend. In his second speech in Book 18
he dwells repeatedly on the fact that he was of no use to his friend on
the battlefield; now he tries to be of use to him when it is too late. It
is not enough for him to kill Hector, he must try to punish the corpse
as well; a doubly futile act, for not only is Hector 'dumb earth' but
Patroclus himself can desire nothing but burial, as is made plain by
his ghost in Book 23. In the same book Achilles sacrifices dogs, horses
and even some Trojan prisoners at Patroclus' pyre. That is perhaps
the most shocking act in the *Iliad*, and this time it is not a proper part
of Achilles' greatness. 'He devised bad deeds in his mind' – that is the
most literal translation of Homer's words at this point (176). This need
not be a moral condemnation: 'bad' may mean 'unpleasant for the
victims', and Hammond's translation is right to be scrupulously
neutral: 'for the grim purpose he had for them'. But it is as though a
moral judgement threatens to break through at this point, ruffling the
objective surface of Homer's language; and we shall be shocked at
human sacrifice in any case, even if we are not told to be, just as we
are touched by the many little vignettes about the lives of dead
warriors, though there is no overt tug at the heart-strings.

And these killings are futile – that is the point. They would make
sense if the *Iliad* had a belief in the afterlife like that of the Egyptians:
the great man will need furniture, horses, slaves in the next life, and
therefore they are buried with him. The grim pathos of Achilles' act

lies in the poem's rejection of such beliefs: he acts as though he could go on doing something for Patroclus, but he cannot. Death is absolute, and there is no comfort, no palliation.

Though the slaughter beside Patroclus' corpse troubles us, we have seen that there is a greatness in Achilles' very ferocity. Does this mean that the quieter virtues – pity, gentleness – are cast aside? No, it does not. Hector and Patroclus are both praised for gentleness of thought and word (24. 772; 19. 300). Apollo says that Achilles has lost pity (24. 44), and that is a reproach. Achilles, unbidden, takes two robes and a tunic, part of his ransom for Hector, and offers them to wrap the body, which he lifts with his own hands upon its bier (24. 580ff., 589f.); that is an act of generosity and feeling for Priam, and we admire it as such. So, we may say, the moral issue is simple: men ought to show pity, Achilles does not show pity, therefore Achilles is morally at fault. But again we must be careful not to intrude our own beliefs. Pity is a good thing, the poem seems to say, but if a man does not have pity at a certain time, that may simply be a brute fact about which nothing can be done, and the absence of pity in a hero at some phase of his career may even be a part of his greatness. We should be glad if Lycaon might have been spared, but it would be an insensitive reader who did not see a splendour in the very hardness of Achilles' words to him. The pitilessness seems to be a necessary part of a vision – almost one may say a moral vision – which we may feel to be not only different from other heroes' experience but beyond it. That is an appalling conception, but it is a fundamentally tragic conception, high, austere and unflinching in a fashion not easily grasped by the modern liberal imagination. As we have noticed, the poem's largeness has space for other ways of seeing, ones with which the modern mind may be more comfortable, but they are attributed to heroes whose stature is inferior to Achilles' and whose penetration of mind is less keen.

Chapter 6
The End of the Iliad

It is often observed that Book 24 echoes and mirrors Book 1, in construction and in many details of fact and language. In Book 1 an old man comes with a supplication on behalf of his child and is rejected; in the last book an old man comes with a supplication on behalf of his child and is accepted; the oral technique, with its many repetitions of language, reinforces the mirror effect. These devices have a formal function, shaping the poem into a whole and giving to the last book a sense of completion, but their purpose is not only structural; they also contribute to the poem's moral economy. In Book 1 an assembly and quarrel among men is followed by a quarrel among the assembled gods; in Book 24 settlement of differences between gods is followed by a settlement of differences between two men, Priam and Achilles – a mirror image again. In either case the dispute between the gods is quickly and smoothly resolved (in the first book a bit of crude clowning by Hephaestus is enough to do the trick), but settling mortals' differences is far, far harder. The gods' desires and passions are shallower and more transitory than men's. Men are complex and deep in a way that gods are not; they face challenges and dilemmas from which the gods are exempt. The Chinese are said to have a curse: 'May you live in interesting times.' It is the curse of man to be interesting, as it is the gods' blessing to be flat and simple. Thus man's significance is found in his suffering – once more, a powerfully tragic conception. It is true but superficial to say that the gods serve as light relief from the grimness of the battlefield; their happy frivolity is part and parcel of the tragic vision of the poem as a whole.

It is easy to be sentimental about Priam's meeting with Achilles, but Homer is not sentimental. The encounter is not cosily warm but prickly. Priam supplicates Achilles in the ritual manner, grasping him with his hands. Here the oral technique of repetition and variation has a powerful effect. Throughout the poem there have been supplications to men, every one of them rejected; what will Achilles do? 'He took the old man by the hand and gently pushed him away' (508). 'Pushed away' is the language of rejection; only the qualification 'gently' tells us that Achilles is being kindly, not hard. He accepts, but we feel that it has been a close run thing. The two men 'remember', and weep. They weep together, people say; but that claim, in one sense a truism, is in another profoundly false. Priam weeps for man-slaying Hector, Achilles for Peleus and Patroclus (509ff.). Nowhere perhaps is the ultimate loneliness of the Homeric hero more powerfully seen than in this place, where as the two men weep together, they weep apart; they share the common lot of humanity, which is suffering, but they do not share their particular sorrow.

There is no sympathy, in the strict sense of that word, but there is pity. Achilles raises Priam, pitying his grey hairs, and begins his great speech. It is what Roman rhetoricians were to call a *consolatio*, a speech of comfort; but was ever comfort colder? He reminds Priam that he has killed many of his sons, besides Hector. He says there is no gain in chill lamentation: for 'this is the fate the gods have spun for poor mortal men, that we should live in misery, but they themselves have no sorrows' (525ff.). He sees two old men, Peleus and Priam, both made miserable by his presence at Troy, but there is nothing to be done about it. He ends by telling Priam again to endure and not to mourn, not because there is some consolation, but because there is none: nothing can bring Hector back to life. Achilles is both passionate and dispassionate, warm in his pity for Priam and Peleus, chill in his bare bleak insight into man's inconsolable hopelessness; and it is in the combination of these things that the greatness of the speech lies.

A few moments later a tactless word from Priam has Achilles flaring into anger and threatening to kill his guest; the situation remains tense, not comfortable. But Achilles' nobility asserts itself. After honouring Hector's corpse (as we have seen), he, the man who has refrained from food, now urges Priam to eat. Once more the preparation of a meal is described in phrases of formulaic character, the two men eat and drink, and then at last they can take pleasure in one another's company:

> When they had put away their desire of eating and drinking, then Dardanian Priam gazed at Achilles with admiration for the size of the man and his beauty…And Achilles gazed at Dardanian Priam, admiring his noble looks and the talk that he had heard. When they had taken their pleasure in looking at each other…etc
>
> (628ff.)

Even now the poem will not lapse into easy sentiment: there is warmth, but there is also distance. The two men look and hear and admire, as though inspecting a work of art; there is no pretence that there is real friendship or closeness between them. That austerity is impressive.

In the midst of great emotional complexity, Homer does not disdain a humdrum truth: when people have some food and drink inside them, they feel better and more companionable. The ordinary business of life, with its everyday routines and appetites, is valued by the poem. It is not entirely flippant to observe that the *Iliad* ends, after Hector's funeral, in the same way as *Little Black Sambo*, with a splendid meal, a 'glorious feast in the house of Priam'. We are left, finally, with a basic satisfaction, as at the close of a fairy story or a folktale. In the course of the last book we see the common rhythms of life restored. Priam and Achilles, who have refrained from food, now eat and drink. Achilles, who has abstained from sex, despite his mother's urging, is last seen lying with Briseis. He, the hero of the poem, may justly be excluded from its last episode because by that good and natural act his wrath is as fitly buried as Hector's body will be. Hector receives those proper rituals for the dead of which he had been deprived: the women keen over him, the mound is raised, the banquet eaten.

All this may sound comforting indeed; but it is not. The tragic quality of the *Iliad*'s ending lies in the counterpoint between the goodness on the surface of the poem, with the wholesomeness of life's rituals and pleasures reasserted, and the horror that is to come. The gods have fixed the encounter between Priam and Achilles, and though that meeting itself is fully human and natural, the arrangements which lead to it are filled with an air of magic and wonder. It is presented as a unique event, unrepeatable; it will lead nowhere. Achilles sees the uselessness of what he must do, and he sees no escape from it. And worse is to come: Priam will die hideously, Achilles will die, Troy will be destroyed, its men butchered, its women enslaved. In his last words to Achilles, Priam proposes a truce while Hector is mourned: nine days of lamentation, the burial and feast on the tenth day, the raising of a grave-mound on the eleventh, 'and on the twelfth day let us fight again, if that must be' (664ff.). That is the voice of despair. In the procession of days – nine, ten, eleven, twelve – we hear the remorseless march of time. 'If that must be' – in that phrase, light, simple, almost colloquial, we recognise the hopelessness of the wish. At the end of the poem life seems good and man a noble animal – more so than ever; that is why the ending is supremely tragic. As we leave the *Iliad*, the Trojans are feasting, but they are inches from the abyss.

Chapter 7
The Breadth of the Odyssey

The *Odyssey* never refers to the events of the *Iliad*; we meet Achilles' ghost, but hear nothing of his wrath, and Hector is not mentioned at all. Some scholars have therefore argued that the *Odyssey* was composed in complete ignorance of the *Iliad*, but this is unlikely; more plausible is the commoner view that the *Odyssey* consciously measures itself against the earlier work. There are in fact details in the *Odyssey* not easily explained except by reference to the *Iliad*. The god Hermes is always bearded in early Greek art; the beardless Hermes of *Odyssey* 5 seems directly modelled on the beardless Hermes of *Iliad* 24, where the god's extreme youth appears to be an invention fitted to the context, making a contrast with the old man, Priam. A reference to Castor and Polydeuces in the underworld (11. 300ff.) seems to complement or 'correct' a passage of the *Iliad* discussed in Chapter 2: though the life-giving earth holds them, they are still alive; and the *Iliad*'s unique phrase, *phusizoos aia*, is repeated to complete the allusion. In a loose sense the *Odyssey* carries the *Iliad*'s story onward, and it may be significant that most of the tales of the Trojan War told within it belong to the war's last phase.

More important than these details is the scheme of the poem as a whole. Aristotle famously pointed out that the *Iliad* handles a single action. The title *Iliad* (that is, Troy Story) is a misnomer; the subject is the wrath of Achilles, just one episode in the tenth year of the war. The action takes less than a month, and most of that time passes in the first and last books, which are symmetrically planned in this respect; twenty-one books cover three days only, an astonishing combination of expansion and concentration.

This is an extraordinary conception; and it is surely in emulation of the *Iliad* that the *Odyssey* fits it to a story to which it seems less naturally suited. At the start the *Odyssey* announces that its subject is a man who wandered far, who saw the cities of many men and learnt their mind, and suffered much upon the sea. That suggests a tale of picaresque adventure, which is indeed the instinctive idea that most of us have of the poem, but in fact the *Odyssey* is not the story of the hero's wanderings. Instead, it is a story of *nostos* (return home): how Odysseus came home and slew the suitors. That is essentially a single action, covering no more time than the events of the *Iliad*; and to fit this conception, the ten years of Odysseus' wanderings are told in flashback. This device enables the poet to combine two different types of adventure story, the heroic and the fantastic, and also to vary the objective manner inherited from the *Iliad* with a narrative told in the first person. As we shall see, one of the pleasures of the *Odyssey* is the way that it juxtaposes different tones or different kinds of story.

If the *Odyssey* emulates the *Iliad* in its construction, in other respects it seems designed to contrast with it. Broadly and crudely speaking, the *Odyssey* tends to be inclusive, the *Iliad* exclusive; the *Iliad* focuses and the *Odyssey* diffuses. An example of this difference can be seen in the settings of the two works; for whereas the *Odyssey* imitates the older poem in its use of time, it contrasts in its use of place. The human actors in the drama of the *Iliad* are confined to the city and plain of Troy, except for a brief journey to an island off the coast in the first book. Even the gods are fairly restricted in their movements: they are usually to be found near the battlefield, or gathered on Olympus, or else travelling between these two sites. Thanks to Homer, the idea of the gods being collected together in one place became very familiar, but it may well have been an invention of the *Iliad*, or of the particular tradition of which the *Iliad* is the culmination. Much of what we know about Greek religion suggests that the gods had their separate habitations and spheres of influence. The gathering of men and even gods into small areas is part of the *Iliad*'s drive towards compression and concentration.

The hero of the *Odyssey*, however, is a traveller. When we first meet him, he is on Calypso's isle of Ogygia, which lies far out in the Ocean. He is at the edge of the world; it is as though Homer wishes to bring him across the largest possible distance in the course of the poem. This broad geography has a moral meaning. Calypso's name is formed from the verb, *kaluptein*, to hide; she is the Concealer. She has kept Odysseus in solitary confinement, so to speak, and 'there is no city of mortal men nearby' (5. 101). But the *Odyssey* is a social poem: whereas the *Iliad* asserts the ultimate loneliness of the hero, the *Odyssey* shows us man embedded in a society and a landscape. Significantly, the most social book of the *Iliad*, the twenty-third, is the one closest to the *Odyssey*'s tone of good-humoured irony. Odysseus' journey from Ogygia to Ithaca, to his kingdom, his house, his bedroom, is also a journey from isolation towards an ever closer community.

Meanwhile Telemachus is going on his own travels, which are both like and unlike those of his father. The motive for his journey to mainland Greece is pretty casually sketched in. Homer does not want to use Telemachus to advance the plot; instead he takes pleasure, once more, in putting together two different kinds of story so that they touch, but only lightly. He plays with similarity and difference: Telemachus' journey is like Odysseus' in that he is 'going into society'; it is unlike in that he goes out and away from home into a wider world, while his father is returning home from a great distance. Telemachus' story is the ultimate ancestor of what the Germans call the *Bildungsroman*, the novel which describes its hero's growth and development. We could say of him, though Homer does not directly do so, that he too, like Odysseus (1. 3), sees the cities of men and knows their mind. His progress takes him first to Nestor at Pylos, where he meets Peisistratus, a young man of his own age and breeding. The two of them travel on to Menelaus' court at Sparta, represented as more rich and glamorous than Nestor's home: to Telemachus' young eyes it seems like the palace of Zeus himself (4. 74). When he returns to Ithaca, the suitors are struck by his new assertiveness. He asserts himself against his mother too: 'I think and know all in my heart, the good and the bad; before, I was still inexperienced [*nēpios*]' (18. 228ff.). (The word *nēpios* means both 'fool' and 'baby'.) Eventually, he will order Penelope to her room, and she will obey in amazement, 'for she laid her son's shrewd saying to her heart' (21. 355). Telemachus is now a man.

The *Odyssey*'s inclusiveness and its social dimension are also seen in the range of characters portrayed in it, which is much wider than in the *Iliad*. The *Iliad* is a masculine poem, in which the women, except perhaps for Helen, are present to typify some role in relation to their menfolk: as mother, wife or chattel. In one respect the *Odyssey* stays close to the *Iliad*: it does not contain the heroically virtuous or heroically wicked women from Greek myth whom we meet in tragedy: there is no Antigone, Medea or Clytemnestra of the familiar kind. Indeed, the Clytemnestra of the *Odyssey* is subordinated to her lover, in striking contrast to Aeschylus' later treatment of the story in his *Oresteia*, and Nestor even claims that she had excellent sense (3. 266). Apart from Odysseus himself, the more memorable characters are mostly women. Odysseus' girlfriends (if one may so call them) seem designed to portray a range of female types and female styles of affection. Nausicaa's maidenly *tendresse* is in contrast to Calypso, the type of the passionate woman, who contrasts again with Circe, a sort of divinised good-time girl, equally content to turn Odysseus into a pig, have an affair with him, or speed him on his way when he wishes to leave. He also benefits from Athena's sexless affection and Penelope's wifely stoicism.

In the *Iliad* no common soldier speaks except for Thersites in the second book, and he is allowed to utter only to strengthen the moral that the common people should know their place and keep quiet. The *Odyssey*, however, gives prominence even to slaves and beggars. Among those honoured to greet Odysseus in a scene of recognition are not only his wife, son and father, but Eumaeus and the herdsman Philoetius, Eurycleia, a slave woman, and even a dog. The warm pathos of the scene with the dog Argus (17. 291ff.) would be quite out of place in the other poem; indeed the scene closest to it in the *Iliad* is profoundly different in spirit. Achilles' horses weep for Patroclus (17. 426ff.), and Zeus reflects that he should never have given the horses to Achilles' father, for they are ageless and immortal, whereas there is nothing on earth more miserable than man. In other words, though they are only animals, the mere fact of their death-lessness should have kept them separate from any care for men; the loneliness of mankind could hardly have been more acidly expressed. The effect in the *Iliad* is one of isolation, in the *Odyssey* of unity: a whole society, in all its ranks, welcomes Odysseus home, and even a hound has his place in this fellowship.

Chapter 8
The Two Worlds of Odysseus

On the face of it there are two kinds of Odysseus in the poem. There is the folktale figure, the trickster, wily, curious, cheeky, acquisitive, the cousin of Jack the Giantkiller and Sinbad the Sailor; and there is the Odysseus of the *Iliad*, a hero of epic song. The one Odysseus is a wanderer among magic and monsters, the other is a king rooted in his own kingdom, a noble whose prowess is displayed in close combat with other nobles. The co-existence of these two conceptions is due to the tradition. Odysseus the trickster seems to be a very ancient figure; we have stories about his wiles which are quite independent of Homer. At some stage, probably much earlier than the *Iliad*, he becomes attached to the Troy story, but even in the *Iliad* as we have it there are trace-indications of his origins elswhere: he is regarded as belonging to a generation older than that of the other Achaeans, and he belongs to a part of Greece remote from the Mycenaean heartland out of which most of the heroes come.

However, we should not regard the two types of Odysseus as a flaw in the *Odyssey*: on the contrary, the diversity of the tradition is material with which the poet plays, and from which he produces some of his most delicate effects. From one point of view the main narrative itself is a blend of folktale and epic tale: obvious folktale elements are the magic disguise, the wondrous bow that only Odysseus is strong enough to bend, the fantastic way in which one man can kill dozens almost single-handed, the riddle of the bed. But the simple story of Odysseus' homecoming has been expanded to a heroic length comparable to that of the *Iliad*, and that expansion of scale is matched by one of the leading ideas of the poem, the heroisation of the domestic; we shall come back to this in due course.

From another point of view, though, it can be said that the two kinds of Odysseus are kept almost separate. When he tells the story of his wanderings he begins in the real world, with Ismarus in Thrace, Cythera and Cape Malea. From Malea he is carried by a storm for nine days, and that storm blows him right off the map. Thereafter he is in a wholly mythical world, inhabited mainly by gods and monsters,

Fig. 3. Odysseus blinding the one-eyed giant, Polyphemus, was a favourite subject with vase-painters (here on a jar of about 520 BC). The folktale is depicted with appropriately crude gusto. In the poem Odysseus describes how he twisted the stake while his men pushed; adapting the story for visual treatment, the artist has Odysseus at the front thrusting, his foot pressed against Polyphemus' chest.

and otherwise by peoples who are dangerous in magical or exotic ways (the Lotus-Eaters, the cannibal Laestrygonians). The lying stories that Odysseus tells after his return to Ithaca are set in real places, like Crete and Egypt, while the geography of the 'true' adventures that he tells in Phaeacia is entirely fantastic – so far are the two fictional worlds of the *Odyssey* kept apart.

The poet's pleasure in the juxtaposition of these two kinds of fiction comes out above all in the place where they meet, Scheria, land of the Phaeacians, the charm of which resides in the delicate way that it is poised between the familiar and the fantastic. This is a magic place: there are fruit and blossom in Alcinous' garden all the year round (7. 117ff.), there are automata in his palace (7. 91ff., 100ff.); the Phaeacians' ships steer themselves (8. 557ff.); this people, as Alcinous himself says, is especially close to the gods, who come and join their feasts in person (7. 201ff.). But this does not prevent the poet from regarding them with an ironic humour, which like much in the poem is understated: as in the *Iliad*, we are often not told what to think; we make our own deductions. Alcinous, the generous host, proposes that each of the Phaeacian nobles should make Odysseus a present, but spoils the effect by adding that they should recoup the cost from the people later (13. 10ff.). Thus spake Alcinous, 'and the speech pleased them'; the formula acquires an edge in the context.

There are other hints that Alcinous is a bit of a bumbler; for example Nausicaa's advice, unexplained, that when Odysseus enters the palace, he should pass by Alcinous (who 'sits drinking wine like an immortal') and supplicate the queen so that he can get what he wants (6. 308ff.). Later Alcinous presses Odysseus to come and watch the Phaeacians at their sports, so that 'the stranger may tell his friends when he comes home how far we excel others in boxing and wrestling and jumping and running' (8. 101ff.). When Odysseus is goaded into taking part he wins the discus competition easily, and threatens to beat his young rivals at boxing, wrestling and even running as well. Alcinous blandly adjusts his earlier boast; it is another example of how repetition and the formulaic manner can be used, neatly and economically, to humorous effect:

> We are not outstanding boxers and wrestlers, but we run swiftly and are the best of seamen, and always dear to us are feasting, the lyre and dances, changes of clothing, hot baths and bed. But come... make merry, so that the stranger may tell his friends when he comes home how far we excel

others in seamanship, fleetness of foot, dancing and song.
(246ff.)

Well, we may reflect, it takes no great skill to like hot baths and fresh linen. But the passage is not simply comic: there is something touching and lovely in the idyll of Scheria, a land of dance – as we shall see.

Homer's blend of the elevated and the everyday is at its most delicate in the handling of Nausicaa. She belongs with Circe and Calypso in the sequence of women whom Odysseus encounters in his wanderings, but she differs from the others in that they are goddesses, while she is an ordinary mortal, and that they have sexual relations with him, while she may not. She is unlike Circe and Calypso, and yet – here is the delicacy – not wholly unlike. Nausicaa too is physically drawn to Odysseus, and we may start to wonder if her story also will be one of passion and desolation. And though she is not a goddess, at moments she resembles one. As she plays with her maidens she is likened to Artemis, accompanied by her nymphs (6. 102ff.). When Odysseus comes forward to her in supplication, he asks her if she is god or mortal, and makes the comparison with Artemis again (149ff.). This is flattery, to be sure, but flattery with a sort of truth in it. Later, he will promise that when he reaches home, he will always pray to her as to a god, in gratitude for what she has done for him (8. 467f.). The charming naturalism with which Nausicaa's girlhood is portrayed gains a radiance from these hints of divinity that hover about it. One can easily be pompous or sentimental about Nausicaa, which Homer is not; but it is fair to say that Homer shows us that, in a sense, girlishness can be divine.

The preparations for Nausicaa's excursion are a social comedy of hidden motives and tacit understandings. First Athena comes to her, disguised as one of her friends, and urges her to go and wash her clothes in preparation for her marriage, which cannot be far off; the goddess conceals her true purpose, which is to bring Nausicaa face to face with Odysseus (and indeed, since he will be naked, rather more than face to face). Nausicaa, for her part, is embarrassed to talk about marriage to her father, and pretends that she wants to wash his own and her brothers' clothes. In turn, Alcinous recognises her real motive, but goes along with the pretence, as though he had not seen through it. These social levities are also part of a moral vision. Manners makyth man; and a part of good manners, in Homer's idea, is a respect for reticences. A bad host, like the Cyclops, demands Odysseus' name at once (9. 252); the good host Alcinous waits until

Odysseus has been bathed and fed before enquiring about him (8. 550ff.). In the reticences of Athena, Nausicaa and Alcinous there is a mixture of cunning and good feeling; it is part of the ethos of the *Odyssey*, serious but mischief-loving, good-humoured and yet wry, that these two things should come so close together.

After the washing is done, Nausicaa and her maidens play ball. This is not a competition but a dance, accompanied by singing. Nausicaa had told her father that she wanted to do her brothers' laundry because 'they always wish to have newly washed clothes to go to the dance' (6. 64ff.). In the Phaeacians' happy world, order and harmony, which are leading themes of the poem, are lifted out of the solemn business of common life into the playfulness of dancing and music.

The scene of Nausicaa and her maidens is the first picture in European literature of simple happiness. But curiously enough, the washing of clothes had already been associated with the idea of happiness in the *Iliad*. As Achilles chases Hector around the walls of Troy, they pass the washing troughs

> where the Trojans' wives and lovely daughters used to wash their bright clothes, in earlier times, in peace, before the sons of the Achaeans came.
>
> (22. 154ff.)

There, in the midst of horror, is a brief glimpse of the good time that will never return. And surely it is no accident that laundry and pleasure should be twice associated together. Ordinarily, the women's sphere is indoors, the men's outdoors; Nausicaa finds her mother spinning by the hearth, with her handmaids, while her father is outside, on his way to take counsel with the chieftains (6. 51ff.). But when women go to wash clothes, they leave the house, they leave the city ('The washing-troughs are far from the city,' as Athena observes, 6. 40); they are women together, freed from the constraints of the home, without men to see them or command them – the presence of Odysseus is indeed an alarming intrusion.

Having created this feminine idyll, what will Homer do with it? Nausicaa hints to Odysseus that he might become her husband. There is more mild deceit and unspoken meaning. She suggests that as they approach the city, Odysseus should leave her and enter separately for fear of gossip; otherwise, someone may say, 'Who is this tall, handsome stranger with Nausicaa? Where did she find him? He will be her husband' (276ff.). And thus Nausicaa, too modest to announce her name directly, has managed to reveal it by indirection. We seem to be at the beginning of a folktale: the story of the stranger who comes to a far land, performs deeds of prowess and marries the king's daughter. Yet Nausicaa and Odysseus separate before they reach the city, and apart from one very brief scene, apparently of farewell, he seems not to see her again. It is as though the romance has been lost or forgotten before it ever got started.

Odysseus cannot of course marry Nausicaa. The Phaeacians, who have no existence in myth independent of Homer, have plainly been invented to fit into the *Odyssey*, or into a poem close to the one we know. It is therefore hard to believe that there was ever a love story which got lost as the poem developed. Rather, the poem chooses to toy with the folktale motif, to tease our expectations. The beauty lies in understatement. We have almost forgotten Nausicaa when she comes into the hall where Odysseus is feasting with the Phaeacian nobles. She does not even come close to him, but stands by a pillar, at a distance, as befits a woman. And she speaks two lines only: 'Farewell, stranger,' – for she has not learnt so much as his name – 'so that when you are in your homeland you may still remember me, since you owe thanks to me for first saving you' (8. 461ff.). Odysseus briefly thanks her and promises to remember her with honour. That is all; we do not even have her departure from the hall described.

Notice that the restraint is not only in the telling but in the event itself. Many poets would have milked the story of all the pathos that it could yield. All but a very few, even if they did not dwell upon the girl's heartbreak, would at least have implied it. Homer will not even do this. The pathos is there ('She looked admiringly at Odysseus before her eyes'), but it is kept very light. Nausicaa has been happy and Homer will not let that happiness be destroyed. When Virgil alludes to Nausicaa as he introduces Dido, he prepares to transform the idyll into tragedy; but though Dido's story is a masterpiece, we may feel that with the vanishing of Homer's understatement something has been lost. There is a type of literary critic who cannot be content with the depiction of happiness unless the poet is in some way undercutting it or adding troubling overtones. Homer was wiser.

The Phaeacians themselves fade from the picture in a curious way. Odysseus has no parting from them: he wakes up in Ithaca and finds them gone. We ourselves never learn whether their prayers will dissuade Poseidon from raising a mountain above their city, and they actually disappear from our sight in mid-sentence:

> Thus the chiefs and leaders of the people of the Phaeacians
> prayed to the lord Poseidon, standing around the altar,
> while Odysseus awoke...
>
> (13. 185ff.)

We shall know them no more; nor will anyone else, for Alcinous has resolved that whereas hitherto they have given everyone passage in their ships, they will never do so to mortal men again. Homer's technique of narrative, in refusing to complete the story, is a strange one, teasing in its elusiveness; but it is curiously apt that the Phaeacians, who have combined the charms of domesticity with the enchantments of distance, should pass from the poem by a mysterious evanescence.

Chapter 9
Homer's Morality

The *Odyssey* stakes out a clear moral position from the start. In the opening lines we learn that Odysseus' companions perished through their own *atasthaliai*, presumptuous acts or recklessness, because they ate the cattle of the Sun, which they had been forbidden to do. The action of the poem begins not among men but on Olympus, and the first speech comes from Zeus himself: the supreme god lays down the ground rules, so to speak, at the outset (32ff.). Men blame the gods, he declares, 'for they say that evils come from us'; but in fact they also suffer troubles beyond their apportionment through their own wrongdoing (*atasthaliai* again). His example is Aegisthus, who in defiance of the gods' express warning, married Agamemnon's wife and killed him upon his return. Therefore Agamemnon's son must take vengeance for his father's death.

That speech is evidently a 'programme' for the poem as a whole. Aegisthus has committed two crimes, adultery and murder, and these are the crimes which in effect the suitors are hoping to commit. We hear several times of Clytemnestra, Agamemnon's faithless wife, and Agamemnon's ghost explicitly contrasts her with the example of a good wife, Odysseus' own Penelope (11. 444ff.). Recurrent in the poem is the idea of *peira*, testing; throughout the *Odyssey* men and women are on their mettle, so to speak. In the *Iliad* the idea that the gods have a general oversight of men's behaviour is not totally absent, but it is almost always kept out of view; in the *Odyssey* it becomes more prominent. This shift in emphasis is matched by a change in the way the gods are presented: as they become more concerned with how men conduct themselves, they become less remote. In the *Iliad* we commonly feel that the barrier between gods and men is absolute; but Odysseus' wanderings take him among minor deities who get caught up in the affairs of men, and can be mutilated, grieved or bested by a mere mortal. In the *Iliad* there is no important deity of this kind other than Thetis, and she is indeed felt to be an exception within the poem: because she feels true grief, she is ashamed to come among the immortals on Olympus, where grief does not belong (24. 90ff.). The 'cast list' of Olympian gods in the *Iliad* is quite large; the *Odyssey* cuts it down. Though Hermes has a significant supporting role in two books, only Zeus, Athena and Poseidon play a really important part in the story. Athena's constant presence, guiding and protecting, is among the chief reasons why the poem's tone, as a whole, is that of a comedy; though so much of the *Odyssey* tells of suffering and endurance, we know that she is on hand to keep an eye on things and bring the adventure to a predestinately happy end. And she has a kind of intimacy with Odysseus such as would be unthinkable in an Olympian within the *Iliad*. When Odysseus has landed on Ithaca, she teases him by appearing disguised as a herdsman and allowing him to tell her a lying story. The trickster has been tricked: Athena smiles, and grasps him with her hand, and declares delightedly that even a god would need to be crafty to outwit him (13. 287ff.). She takes a pleasure in his society which is something close to friendship: at this point she does not appear as the aegis-bearing warrior maiden of the *Iliad* but joins Circe, Calypso, Nausicaa and Penelope in the company of the women who care for him.

It may seem that the *Odyssey* is a moral poem in a way that distinguishes it from the *Iliad*. In a sense that is true, in a sense not. The *Iliad* is undergirded by a stern morality. Adultery is raised as an issue at the start of the *Odyssey*, but from the *Iliad* we learn that adultery has been enough to cause the whole Trojan War. Occasionally we are reminded of a knowledge which the Achaeans and the Trojans seem to share, though they and we often forget it: that in the end Troy must fall, because, as Diomedes puts it, 'god is with us in our mission here' (9. 49). This can hardly mean anything other than that Zeus will ensure the ultimate victory of the Achaeans because the Trojans are in the wrong: they are accessories to Paris' adultery. In Book 4 the Trojan Pandarus breaks the truce which the two sides have just made – an impious breach of an oath. Shortly afterwards he is killed; the poet makes no comment, but we infer that his impiety has been punished. This small episode represents the entire war in microcosm: it reinforces our awareness that the Trojans, however sympathetic, are morally in the wrong position.

One school of thought denies Zeus a moral function in the *Iliad*. On this account he is merely upholding his own *timē* (honour), just as Achilles does: he is the god of hospitality; Paris has breached the laws of hospitality by abducting his host's wife; Zeus will therefore avenge the insult done to himself. (Zeus' action would thus be equivalent to

Apollo's in *Iliad* Book 1, where the god sends the plague on the Greeks not because Agamemnon has ill-treated an old gentleman but because the old gentleman is Apollo's own priest.) But there is no incompatibility between saying that Zeus upholds his honour as the god who oversees hosts and guests and that Zeus exercises a moral function; these are two views of the same supposed fact. The way that a moral role is built into a fundamentally timocratic (honour-based) conception of the gods is precisely by making them patrons of some area of moral action.

The salient feature of the *Iliad* is not that it has no morality but that it does not make open moral judgements. Its objectivity is deeply impressive: on the one hand the poet becomes invisible and we see each action plain and clear, on the other we become aware of a controlling moral vision. If those two things seem to be contradictory, the answer is, 'Read the *Iliad* and see.' The *Odyssey* is different not because its author inhabits a different moral universe but because it is a different kind of poem. The disguised Odysseus tells Penelope that in the land of a good king the black earth bears wheat and barley, the flocks are fertile, the sea affords fish in plenty and the people prosper (19. 109ff.). We need not suppose that the poet of the *Odyssey* believed this to be literally true; such a faith would have been hard to sustain in the Dark Age of Greece. A better guide might be Miss Prism's description of her novel in *The Importance of Being Earnest*: 'The good ended happily, and the bad unhappily. That is what Fiction means.' The *Odyssey* has this in common with the *Iliad*: it is a fiction, that is, a making, a specially constructed world. But in place of the *Iliad*'s tragic plainness, its ultimate blank hopelessness, it offers the consolations of secure moral judgement. It is a comedy – a story in which the good end happily and the bad unhappily – and it divides its characters into the good and the bad as part of its exploration of the *comédie humaine*.

The moral strictness of the *Odyssey* is the servant and not the enemy of comedy, as one might expect, because though the poem is moral it is not moralistic. A work with a strong moral content may be strenuously earnest; we surely feel the *Aeneid* to be like that. But equally, stories that divide people firmly and clearly into good and bad may be entertainments or escapes from reality – fairy-tales, for instance, or westerns. The *Odyssey* is a serious poem, but it has the wit to express its seriousness through the artifices of fable and fantasy. Some of the 'tests' have a folktale quaintness: Odysseus' testing of

Laertes, for example, or the tests by which Penelope comes to recognise that the stranger is truly her husband. But the moral test is also a serious one. The touchstone is above all the treatment of strangers and beggars, who are especially under the protection of Zeus. *xeinos* means both guest and stranger, *xenie* is hospitality, and *xeineia* are gifts made to a guest; the *xein-* words come again and again in the poem. The test here is not, like the challenge to the heroes in the *Iliad*, something for aristocrats only, but one by which people of all kinds can be judged. The Cyclops, the suitors, the goatherd Melanthius and the beggar Irus all treat Odysseus insultingly; conversely, the king Alcinous and the swineherd Eumaeus are both examples of the good host. The formulaic method brings out the social range of this morality. Nausicaa tells her handmaids to take care of Odysseus, 'For all strangers and beggars are from Zeus, and giving is a small thing and welcome [*dosis d'olige te phile te*]' [6. 207ff.]. Eumaeus echoes these phrases with a heavy emphasis on the repeated *xeinos*, 'stranger':

> Stranger, it is not right for me to dishonour a stranger, even if one inferior to you should come; for all strangers and beggars come from Zeus and giving *such as mine* is a small thing and welcome [*dosis d'oligē te philē te gignetai hēmeterē*].
>
> (14. 56ff.)

The small changes in the last phrase shift the meaning: royal Nausicaa says that kindness to strangers costs little; Eumaeus, the swineherd, says that he has only little to give. But the similarities of language remind us that the slave is as courteous as the princess.

The *Odyssey* remains a deeply aristocratic poem in that loyalty is a supreme virtue in the lowly; the disloyal, like Melanthius or the faithless maidservants, are savagely punished. But that cruelty is the darker side of a conception which gives the humble some sort of moral importance; they suffer because they have failed a test which matters. Thersites, in the *Iliad*, can be dismissed with mere ridicule; Melanthius cannot. The *Odyssey*, indeed, surrounds humble and domestic things with a kind of heroic seriousness. The nobility themselves perform everyday tasks: a princess does the washing, and Odysseus, rebuking an insulting suitor, implies that he is experienced at mowing and ploughing as well as in the arts of war (18. 366ff.). Conversely, even slaves may be granted their own dignity. A considerable proportion of the *Odyssey* passes in Eumaeus' home, and that fact in itself says something about the poem's values. The leisurely pace of the narrative here is not a fault in the poem, but the proper expression of its care for everyday things. The formulae describe both Eumaeus, though he has only four slaves under him, and the herdsman Philoetius as 'leader of men', and Eumaeus is also the 'noble swineherd'; these phrases, though quaint, are not meaningless. Eumaeus' swine live in a kind of pig palace, built of quarried stone, in a place which commands a wide view, with a courtyard, and with the females penned apart from the boars (14. 5ff.). This is an example of the orderliness which is one of the poem's ideals. Now the extreme symmetry of Alcinous' garden represents the order which reigns in his palace; it stands in contrast to the confusion in Odysseus' palace, occupied by the disorderly, wenching suitors. From one point of view Alcinous' and Odysseus' palaces have more in common with one another than they have with a piggery; from another, Eumaeus is the one person on Ithaca who has achieved the handsome, dignified order which we met in Scheria.

He is not, indeed, entirely an ordinary swineherd, for we learn that he is of royal birth, but was kidnapped by pirates as a child; however, that fact has its own significance. He is one more example of that doubleness in which the poem delights. Scheria was both a fairy-tale kingdom and a recognisable, ordinary society; Eumaeus is both a prince and a slave. His noble ancestry represents that blend of the grand and the humble which is one of the poem's charms.

Chapter 10
Landscape, Man and Society in the *Odyssey*

Like Odysseus himself, the *Odyssey* is wide-ranging and enquiring; it is curious about the world, and that curiosity extends beyond an interest in diverse peoples to an interest in a variety of landscapes also. A complete picture of a society should include its setting, and indeed that setting may tell us something about the people who inhabit it. Partly this is a practical matter: when Odysseus comes to a new place, he is anxious to know whether it is occupied by monsters or savages or by 'men that live by bread', and he looks at the scenery for evidence of cultivation. A pleasing landscape is one of pasture, tilth and vineyards. Here practical and aesthetic considerations seem to come together: a cultivated landscape is welcoming because it gives signs of civilization, and it is also pleasing to the eye for that very reason.

The Cyclopes live on an island where there are well watered meadows by the shore (9. 132ff.), good soil, as Odysseus remarks, for vines and corn, but Polyphemus himself chooses to live instead in a cave among wooded mountains. In a sense this is perfectly realistic: Polyphemus wants to live in 'solitude and lawlessness', and naturally this takes him away from the fertile coastlands into a landscape of another kind. But the *Odyssey* constantly presses beyond simple realism, and Homer goes on to give the Cyclops a unity with his landscape that is poetic and imaginative. His cave is high, with lofty oaks and pines around it; he is himself of monstrous size, like a wooded peak among high mountains, which stands out solitary, apart from the other hills (9. 181ff.). Here the simile and the actual scenery and the monster himself are fused into one amalgam.

Odysseus' lady-friends, too, are found each in a landscape appropriate to herself. Circe, deceitful, uncivilised, yet a smooth woman of the world, lives in a palace of polished stone in the midst of an island covered in forest and thick brushwood. The innocent, virginal Nausicaa is seen by the fair stream of the river, where the lively water wells up in abundance, pure and never failing; on the banks the grass grows lush and honey-sweet (6. 85ff.). Meanwhile, the shipwrecked Odysseus, naked and caked in brine, is hidden in the tangles of thick brushwood, and when he steps forth he is like a mountain -bred lion (130). All this is natural and unforced; yet at the same time, the contrast between Odysseus' setting here and Nausicaa's clarifies the contrast between male and female, happiness and misfortune, innocence and experience.

The poem's longest and richest landscape description is of Calypso's setting (5. 57ff.). It appeals to the senses of sound and smell as well as sight. There is something wild about Calypso: in a world of palaces, she, though a goddess, dwells in a cave. Her melodious song mingles with the cry of birds; the cave is aromatic with burning cedar and juniper. Around its mouth runs a vine, rich with clusters; four springs flow with clear water, and around are soft meadows, blooming with parsley and violet. A wood surrounds the cave, not thicket as on Circe's island, but a luxurious blend of alder, poplar, and sweet-smelling cypress.

This is a landscape fit for the Concealer. Even within her island she is hidden: her song and the fragrance of burning wood come from within the cave and are seen from without (a distinctive feature of the scene is that it is observed from an individual's viewpoint, that of the god Hermes who sees and marvels). The vine and the grove alike push Calypso away from the immediate field of vision, deep into an unseen interior. Obscurely and powerfully we feel that this setting, both dark and luxuriant, thick with leaves and flowers, heavy with fruitage, is the landscape of passion.

The idea has entered the poem that in some way landscape may reflect the character of men and women, even that it may be responsive to human vice and virtue: as we have seen, in the land of a good king the crops are heavy and the flocks fertile. These fancies are linked to another idea which is emotional and yet more down to earth: a feeling for what may be called the particularity of a known landscape. When Alcinous asks Odysseus who he is, Odysseus gives his name, and goes on to say that he lives on Ithaca; he then gives us a little geography, naming Ithaca's mountain and three more islands nearby, and describing how they lie in relation to one another (9. 19ff.). The point of this description is that it is individualised: this particular pattern of islands is distinctive and unique. And Odysseus gives the description as part of his personal identity; it is what the Greeks called a *sphragis* or seal (the modern equivalent might be a signature or perhaps a fingerprint). He admits that Ithaca is 'rough, but a good nurse of young men; as for myself, I can think of no sweeter sight than a man's own land' (9. 27f.). The sentiment is not very far from 'a poor thing but mine own'. Ithaca is not especially rich or beautiful, but Odysseus desires it above all things because it is his, it is where he belongs.

This bears a relation to the way that he feels about Penelope. He grants to Calypso that she, a goddess, is more beautiful than his wife; but even though Calypso offers him immortality, he prefers to leave. 'Even so, I wish and long every day to come home and see the day of my return' (5. 219ff.). Scholars have debated over Odysseus and Penelope. Does the poem offer a high, even romantic view of marriage? Or does Odysseus essentially want to recover what belongs to him – a package which includes his rank, his possessions and his wife? If we consider the wholeness of the *Odyssey*, its balance between society and the individual, we may be able to answer yes to both questions. Let us look closer.

And to begin, let us raise two other questions that have troubled scholars. First, why is it so hard for Penelope to recognise Odysseus, when Argus, Eurycleia and the rest have no difficulty? Secondly, there seem to be traces left in the poem of a variant version in which Odysseus revealed himself to Penelope before he killed the suitors. If this is correct, what effect do they have on the work's meaning and coherence?

In facing the second question, we should remember that an oral poet cannot retract anything that he has sung, and a poet raised in an oral tradition may well tend to accumulate rather than cancel his material. Lines composed for a variant may well be retained unless they are flatly incompatible with the final version. (A plausible example of the process is at *Iliad* 16. 49ff., where one part of Achilles' speech might naturally imply (though it does not necessitate) that there had been no embassy to him, while another part makes no sense unless there has been one.) What we have to consider is the effect in the poem as we have it. From this point of view there is a curiously moving tension between the Penelope who knows nothing and the Penelope who sometimes behaves as though she did know. Odysseus' mere presence in the house somehow illuminates her, even though she is unaware of it. A kind of hilarity invades her: even before Odysseus reaches the palace, she speaks of her hopes for his return; Telemachus sneezes, and she laughs at the happy omen (17. 528ff.). Once Odysseus is in the house, Athena makes Penelope's spirit urge

her, as it never has before, to display herself to the suitors and to make
their hearts flutter with hope, so that she may win more honour from
her son and husband; and she laughs at her idle thought (18. 158ff.).
Through some instinct that goes beyond reason she warms to the
stranger, and here we can detect Homer deliberately playing with the
idea of a Penelope who does not know and yet behaves like one who
does. '*Dear* stranger,' she says (19. 350ff.), ' – for of all strangers from
afar who have come to my house there has never before been one so
shrewd or *dear...*' (The word translated dear (*philos*) also means 'of
the same family'.) She adds that the stranger is the same age as
Odysseus; surely, we think, she must recognise him at any moment.
But no: Homer is teasing us yet again; Penelope withdraws, and
Eurycleia takes her place to effect the recognition. Yet even Eurycleia
seems to know unconsciously before she knows in truth: in her speech
(19. 363ff.) she addresses someone whom she calls 'you'. At first it is
the absent Odysseus, then the stranger before her; it is as though she
has already sensed that the two men are one and the same.

Penelope's trouble in recognising Odysseus for who he is cannot
of course be explained in naturalistic terms; it has another meaning.
Now Odysseus has told Nausicaa (6. 182ff.) that there is nothing better
than when man and woman dwell together with their minds in har-
mony. This brings pain to their enemies, joy to their friends; but they
best know the truth of it themselves (*malista de t'ekluon autoi*). In
prosaic terms, marriage has both a social and a private dimension;
and at the heart of it is an inner knowledge between man and wife
which is maybe beyond description. Married love is indeed notor-
iously hard to depict, and it is revealing that perhaps the two greatest
works of art to celebrate or explore it, the *Odyssey* and Mozart's *Magic
Flute*, do so through the medium of symbol and fantasy. There is a
resemblance between the culminations of the *Iliad* and the *Odyssey*:
in both the hero is healed through the sexual act; in both a public
restoration is followed by a private one; and in both the private
reconciliation is the more complex and difficult because in the end it
is the more important. It is appropriately harder for Penelope to
recognise Odysseus than it is for Argus or Eurycleia because so much
more is at stake: the relationship is deeper. It is significant, too, that
the trick or test which finally brings Odysseus and Penelope together
is to do with their marriage bed. The test, which has been the mark of
man as a social animal, is finally turned towards the most private part
of himself. In the *Odyssey*'s vision there is no conflict between

Odysseus wanting his rank and wealth back and Odysseus wanting Penelope for herself, because he is the head of a society in which family, household, property, people and land are part of one whole. Moreover, the harmonious man knows no boundary between possession and affection: Odysseus wants to see Ithaca again both because it is his and because it is a particular remembered landscape, and he wants to see Penelope again both because she is his and because she is a particular remembered woman.

His *nostos* is complete. In their bed, after he and Penelope have made love, he tells her the story of his adventures (the poet provides a summary; we note wryly that Circe and Nausicaa are left out). And thus the whole breadth of his experience is brought into a narrow room and taken into the heart of his marriage. But: *malista de t'ekluon autoi* – and we can perhaps follow them no further.

Fig. 4. Odysseus and the Sirens, from a jar of about 480 BC. This is the inquiring Odysseus, the seeker after experience. Bound to the mast, he listens to the Sirens' dangerously beautiful song; his crew row on, their ears stopped with wax. This vase-painting inspired J.W. Waterhouse's picture, Ulysses and the Sirens *(1891), now in the National Gallery of Victoria, Melbourne.*

Chapter 11
Secondary Epic

Homer was the best of all poets – the ancient world was agreed on that. When Ennius, whom the Romans were to regard as their first great poet, wrote his *Annals*, he imagined Homer appearing in a dream to instruct him; but the subject of his poem, Roman history, was utterly unlike Homer's. In the *Aeneid*, by contrast, Virgil chose to parallel the two Homeric epics; roughly speaking, the first six books echo the *Odyssey* and the last six the *Iliad*, though one large episode in the first half, the memorial games for Anchises in Book 5, is modelled on the *Iliad*, while in the second half, Book 8 is based more loosely on scenes from the *Odyssey*. The whole of Roman literature was written under the shadow of Greece; from the Greeks the Roman poets derived their genres, metres, mythology, figures of speech, and much more besides. The idea of imitation was well understood and accepted: Horace is proud to tell us that he has shown Archilochus and Alcaeus to Rome; Propertius proclaims himself the Roman Callimachus.

Yet Virgil had some people foxed. Suetonius' life of the poet tells us that a number of detractors accused him of plagiarising and complained especially that he had pilfered from Homer. He replied that they should try carrying out the same thefts: they would find that it was easier to filch the club from Hercules than a line from Homer. All of which is enough to show that Virgil's procedure was considered unusual. And his riposte, which may well be authentic and if not is *ben trovato*, suggests how hard the task was that he had set himself: anyone who imitates Homer is in danger of seeming feeble and second-rate by comparison. There is little point in imitation on this scale unless it is a means of saying something new: we should expect to find Virgil using Homer as a means of drawing out the differences between his story and those of the *Iliad* and *Odyssey*. That is a tricky game to play, and a sense of struggle, of difficulty, is at the heart of the *Aeneid*. It is shared between the poet and his hero: Virgil wrestles with his mighty predecessors, and Aeneas toils under the burden laid upon him by Jupiter's plan. 'So great was the toil to found the Roman race,' we are

53

told at the close of Virgil's introduction (1. 30). The theme returns at the end of the eighth book, when Aeneas raises the shield that Vulcan has made for him, 'hoisting on his shoulder the glory and destiny of his descendants' (8. 731). Here symbol and actuality come magnificently together: literally, Aeneas raises a heavy weight of metal on which are depicted scenes from the future history of Rome; figuratively, he bears the burden of working for generations yet to come.

In *1066 and All That* there is a spoof examination paper with the instruction, 'Do not write on both sides of the paper at once.' In a way the *Aeneid* is a refusal to obey that command. Virgil tries to cram everything in. He reworks both the *Iliad* and the *Odyssey*, as it were, but in a poem which is less than the length of either. Rome was unusual among cities in having two foundation myths, the Trojan story and the story of Romulus; Virgil again manages, more or less, to include both, for though he says little directly about Romulus, he builds into his story of Aeneas many things that look forward to the early history of Rome. Indeed, there were two types of model for epic, the mythological and the historical. The *Iliad*, the *Odyssey* and the *Argonautica* of Apollonius of Rhodes draw on heroic myth, but the Greeks also wrote epics about historical events, and Ennius' *Annals* and Naevius' *Punic War* had followed this pattern, telling of stirring deeds in Rome's past. When Virgil first contemplated writing an epic he seems to have expected that it would be largely historical; at least, in the opening of the third book of his *Georgics* he refers to a future poem which will celebrate Augustus' career, though it will also delve into the past, as far as the Troy story. In the event, as we know, he turned this idea on its head, and wrote a poem on the distant past with glances forward to Augustus. But what both conceptions have in common is a fusion of the historical and mythological.

Indeed, his strongly historical imagination is one of the respects in which Virgil differs most plainly from Homer. He shows us this through the shield of Aeneas, so unlike its literary model in the shield of Achilles in *Iliad* Book 18. Modern historians distinguish 'diachronic' and 'synchronic' history. Diachronic history is history as traditionally conceived: the narrative of events and changes through time. Synchronic history is the study of things that change slowly or not at all: for example, structures of economy, society and belief. The shield of Achilles is synchronic history: it depicts timeless features of human society – war, the administration of justice, a festival, and so on. Virgil replaces this with diachronic history: a narrative of Rome that drives through the centuries from Romulus to Augustus.

Critics use the terms 'primary' and 'secondary' epic. Primary epic is the sort of heroic poetry that grows naturally out of a comparatively primitive society: the *Iliad*, the *Odyssey*, *Beowulf*, the *Nibelungenlied* are examples. Secondary epic, such as the *Aeneid* or *Paradise Lost*, is the product of much more advanced and sophisticated societies, in which heroic verse is no longer a natural outgrowth; such poems are accordingly less spontaneous and more artificial, and extremely hard to bring off successfully. Secondary epic tends to be weightier and more moral than primary epic; it deals more obviously with 'great issues'. Whereas Achilles and Odysseus are essentially free spirits, acting for themselves, the actions of the heroes in secondary epic – Aeneas and Adam and Eve – concern far more than themselves, and the destinies of unborn generations hang upon them.

Fig. 5. The Altar of Peace in Rome (13-9 BC) shares something of Virgil's spirit. Here Aeneas, on his arrival in Latium, sacrifices to the household gods which he has brought from Troy. He appears not as a brilliant young hero but as sober, bearded and responsible. His dress recalls statues of Roman kings, a reminder that his actions are laden with significance for future history.

There is much truth in all of this, and the distinction between primary and secondary epic is a useful tool for the critic. But in a way it is misleading, for it conceals the extent to which the characteristics attributed to secondary epic were Virgil's own invention. Plenty of poets, in later Greece and in Rome, wrote epic poems without a sense either that the task was hideously difficult or that every deed of the hero was portentous with large significance. That is Virgil's idea; and if later poets, like Milton, pick it up, it is because of Virgil's influence.

A key term in the *Aeneid* is the adjective *pius* along with the related noun *pietas*. Contained within *pietas* are the ideas of virtue, duty, loyalty, responsibility – duty to one's family, to one's people and to the gods. Aeneas is repeatedly called *pius*; he even introduces himself with the words 'I am *pius* Aeneas' (1. 378). It is the constant awareness of duty and responsibility that makes Aeneas a new kind of epic hero, and which gives his heroism a kind of austerity. In the *Aeneid* Virgil's manner matches his theme: in contrast to Homer's seeming spontaneity, he fashions his poem very carefully and laboriously, always aware of the weight of literary precedent laid upon him; and his hero toils under the burden of destiny.

Chapter 12
Dido and Creusa

We shall now look closer to see how Virgil's 'secondariness' works in practice. We can see the *Aeneid* in terms of the ingenious remodelling of literary materials or as a study of human passions. It is part of Virgil's genius to make these different aspects of his poem interact. Let us see how this works in the case of Dido's story.

Dido parallels at least three heroines from the *Odyssey*, but in fact the closest model for Virgil's narrative comes in an episode from the *Argonautica* of Apollonius, a third-century poet who himself had the *Odyssey* in mind. In the course of their voyage the Argonauts, led by Jason, arrive at the island of Lemnos, where the women have killed all the men and now find that they are missing something in consequence. The appearance of a boatload of manly Argonauts is therefore a godsend. The queen, Hypsipyle, proposes to Jason that he should become king and settle in Lemnos with his men (this is the model for Dido's offer in *Aeneid* Book 1); he declines, but none the less sleeps with her. Heracles, taking the part given in the *Aeneid* to Mercury, chides the men for preferring dalliance to the quest for renown. Jason makes no answer; Hypsipyle sheds tears, but is evidently not deeply or permanently affected; Jason observes that if she should prove to give birth to a son, she should send him to his grandfather when he grows up. And that is that.

If we now turn to the *Aeneid*, we see at once that Virgil has transformed this light, elegant material into the stuff of tragedy. Once Jason has left Lemnos, Hypsipyle can be entirely forgotten, but Aeneas will still be haunted by Dido – more or less literally, since he will meet her in the underworld. The idea of a possible child – which is never allowed to arise at all in the case of Odysseus' liaisons with Circe and Calypso – becomes poignant in the *Aeneid*. At the end of the first speech in which she denounces Aeneas, Dido declares that if only her lover had left her with a little Aeneas, who could recall his father to her memory, she would not feel so helplessly abandoned (4. 327ff.). For 'little', Virgil gives her a colloquial word, *parvulus*, departing momentarily from the dignity appropriate to epic language.

Our understanding of Dido is enlarged: a speech that began as high tragic rhetoric collapses into a tender, plaintive domesticity. We realise that Dido is not only a proud queen but also, with some part of her being, an ordinary woman with ordinary hopes and desires.

We may perhaps say that Dido aspires to be a Penelope: she does not want simply to have an affair with Aeneas; she wants to be his wife and bear his child. But the figure from Homer whom she most resembles is Calypso. This comparison too includes a contrast: Calypso truly loves Odysseus, but she is not shattered when she is forced to give him up, and being a goddess, she is allowed to maintain her dignity even in defeat. She pretends to Odysseus that she is letting him go of her own free will, and he does not see through the deceit. There are no such softenings to Dido's pain.

Virgil also implies a comparison with Nausicaa. When Aeneas first catches sight of Dido, she is likened to the goddess Diana surrounded by her nymphs (1. 498ff.); the simile is borrowed from the *Odyssey* (6. 102ff.), where Nausicaa is likewise compared to Artemis (of whom Diana was the Roman equivalent). The Homeric allusion presents Dido to us, on her first appearance, as young, happy, and beautiful, and because that allusion, once more, includes contrast as well as likeness, it is especially touching. As we have seen, it is the essence of Nausicaa's story that Odysseus will not destroy her happiness; in the case of Aeneas and Dido the outcome will be miserably different.

The comparison with Diana, and by implication with Nausicaa, is the more troubling in its context, for it comes after a beautiful but faintly sinister scene (1. 314ff.). Aeneas meets a young woman (or so she seems) with the face and costume of a Spartan maiden (the word *virgo*, maiden, is much stressed). We know, though Aeneas does not, that this is really his mother Venus, magically disguised. Mysteriously, Aeneas senses that she is a supernatural being: Are you Diana, he asks, or one of the nymphs? But she conceals her identity, and only as she leaves him does he realise who she is. It is clear that she is attractive physically, and Virgil seems especially interested in her legs: he notes how they are revealed by her dress, girt up, and Venus herself draws attention to her purple boots, tied high on her calves (people think that Virgil is too high and solemn to think about such things, but they are mistaken). Now there is something uneasy about these prettinesses: a sexy virginal mother is a troubling thought. And this person, who looked like the virgin goddess Diana, is in fact the goddess of sexual passion. So when Dido is in turn likened to Diana, we may shudder. There is something slithery in Virgil's imagination; when he borrows Nausicaa's simile, the innocent brightness of the Homeric vision has already been stained.

The Homeric background to the *Aeneid* enables Virgil to explore his characters through what can be called a prismatic method. He walks round his men and women, examining them in different lights, or from different aspects. In the course of the poem Aeneas himself is compared, explicitly or implicitly, with many other figures (not all of them Homeric, not all even mythological): with Achilles, Hector, Odysseus, Hercules, Theseus, Jason, Augustus. This is not to say that he is 'identified' with any of these other characters; indeed, the comparisons may be misleading or deceitful. When Aeneas' enemies liken him to Paris, they are dishonest: he is not a seducer, lusting after Lavinia, in fact he has never so much as set eyes on her. And with every one of these comparisons, it remains possible that the unlikenesses may be as important as the likenesses; the comparisons are meant to start our imaginations working, to get us to ask ourselves questions, not to give us pat answers.

So it is with Dido's tragedy. One or two literary echoes remind us of Jason, who cast off Medea, and Theseus, who deserted Ariadne. But it is a bad mistake to say, 'Aha – so Aeneas is in the wrong.' Virgil's allusions start our enquiry, they do not close it. This is a morally serious poem, and the passing allusion cannot be produced, like the proverbial rabbit from the hat, to solve a moral problem in an instant. We have to ask, 'Did Aeneas do wrong, as Jason did? Or is it rather Aeneas' misfortune that he, an honourable man, should have the taint of Jason's dishonour attached to him?'

It would be better to think of Aeneas and Dido as Homeric characters out of their depth. Obscurely, guilt and misery seem to surround their affair from the start; and yet if we look at Virgil's models in Homer and Apollonius, we may ask what is wrong with it. When a travelling hero meets a queen or goddess, he is entitled to a dalliance with her, and no blame attaches to either party. One answer has been to claim that Virgil is imposing the morality of his own time on to his epic story, but this is nonsense. Even if it were true that the Romans of Virgil's day thought it wicked for a widow to remarry (and they did not – Augustus himself had married a widow), Aeneas and Dido themselves belong to a different world, which has it own rules. Virgil has a keen historical imagination, and he goes to some trouble to show us that the time and manners about which he is writing are remote from those of his own age, and that the Trojans are different from the Italians, with certain oriental traits that will be purged from their descendants. In the first book Jupiter unfolds the future, revealing that the events of the *Aeneid* take place centuries before Rome is even founded. Aeneas will rule for three years, his son for thirty, the kings of Alba for three hundred; only then will Rome come into being (265ff.). The lengthening geometrical progression stresses the vast distance between Aeneas and even the first beginnings of the Roman state. The Trojans have a different language, costume and customs from the Italians, and even some of their gods are different.

It is worth dwelling on this matter for a moment, as it has sometimes been much misunderstood. It has been claimed that Aeneas is a 'Roman hero' on the grounds that Anchises addresses him as 'Roman' at the end of his great speech in the underworld (6. 851). But this cannot be right. Aeneas is not a Roman and never will be; and in any case it makes no sense for Anchises to be telling him how to conquer and govern an empire since unlike his Roman descendants he will never be in the business of imperial conquest. These words are not addressed to Aeneas at all. In fact, if we look at the speech as a whole, we shall see that Anchises begins by being solicitous for Aeneas, explaining to him the meaning of the procession of heroes that he sees. But as Anchises' enthusiasm grows, he ceases to speak to Aeneas and forgets him; he asks questions which can only be baffling to his son ('Who could pass you by in silence, great Cato, or you, Cossus?', 6. 841); he begs Julius Caesar, who remains unnamed, not to start the civil war – full of meaning to us, meaningless to Aeneas (834ff.). In the end Anchises' prophetic impetus has built up so much momentum that he projects himself out of his proper time and place to address the Romans of the future – each one of Virgil's readers, citizens of an empire centuries distant in time. This marvellously dramatic conception is wrecked if we take Anchises' last words, in defiance of their sense, to be still directed at his son.

To return to Aeneas and Dido. The moral of Virgil's allusion to earlier epic is that this love affair should have been all right. And so it would have been but for two special circumstances. The first is that Aeneas has a unique task imposed on him by Jupiter; the other is Dido's vow to the dead Sychaeus. That is why Virgil has invented the vow: to surround with an atmosphere of guilt something that would otherwise be guiltless. Does Virgil ever himself say that Dido is guilty of anything? For one moment it may seem that he does:

> No more is Dido moved by how others will see her and
> speak of her, no more does she think of a secret love-affair:
> she calls it marriage, and with this name she adorns her
> fault [*culpa*].

(4. 170-2)

But Virgil's method is frequently subjective; he gets inside his characters and sees things from their point of view, and this may be what he is doing here. The most we can say is that Dido herself feels guilt; whether she deserves to feel this is not a question to which Virgil will give us an easy answer. The tragic paradox of Dido's lot is that it is her nobility which drags her down. A lesser woman would not have sworn the oath, or having sworn it, would have broken it much sooner. Anna, we realise, had she been in Dido's situation, would have climbed into Aeneas' bed without a qualm. We may judge Aeneas similarly: had he been less fine a man, Jupiter would not have laid upon him the burden of founding the Roman race, and his dalliance would have been free of blame. He begins as a Homeric warrior, but somehow he finds himself in a world where the Homeric rules no longer apply.

The story of Dido and Aeneas is a tragedy of incomprehension. She fails to understand that Aeneas, being the man he is, will be bound in the end to follow the course of duty, at whatever cost; he fails to realise that she, being the kind of woman she is, will be utterly wrecked by his loss. Virgil has set the love of Aeneas and Dido, brief, childless and outside the bonds of matrimony, in contrast with the love of Aeneas and Creusa, a settled, married love, blessed with a son. The scene in which Aeneas encounters Creusa's ghost is worth some consideration, not only for the light that it sheds upon his later affair with Dido, but because it is one of the most beautiful and poignant passages in all poetry.

Their meeting shows how for Aeneas even the most basic human situations are caught up in larger issues, for Creusa cannot speak simply to her man, as Andromache or Nausicaa could, about immediate or shared experience; much of her speech must be prophecy of the divine intent. She tells him that he must cross vast tracts of ocean; he will come to the land of Hesperia and the river Tiber, and there a royal bride awaits him (2. 780ff.). A lesser poet would have milked this situation for all it was worth – to think that it is the dead wife who tells Aeneas about the woman who is to succeed her. But Creusa's concern is not to heighten emotion; rather, she tries to damp it down. 'She took away my cares with these words,' Aeneas recalls (775), and we should take what he says seriously. Creusa refers to herself almost entirely in the third person ('It is not allowed for you to take Creusa with you...' and so on), with a sort of detachment. Her purpose is to comfort Aeneas, and it is a tribute to her goodness that, to a degree, she succeeds. We are the more moved by the fact that Creusa tries not to be too moving: the scene is supremely affecting for the very reason that it avoids the tragic note.

Virgil's masterstroke is this: Creusa tells Aeneas not that she loves him but that he loves her: 'Banish your tears for your beloved Creusa' (784). Whereas he and Dido will be mired in mutual incomprehension, Creusa trusts and understands; she can speak of his feelings with confident serenity. Along with Odysseus' words to Nausicaa, this is one of literature's greatest tributes to married love; it is extraordinary to find modern scholars saying that Virgil viewed women with dislike or mistrust. Fittingly, Creusa's last words are not about herself but about her son, and look forward into the future: 'Now farewell, and maintain your love for the son whom we share' (789).

Aeneas never mentions Creusa again, nor does he see her in the underworld. That too has its fitness. A good marriage is complete; its memory does not trouble the spirit, and its value is preserved in the child or children born to it. But Aeneas will learn that he cannot 'finish' with Dido in the same way; that miserable story is not complete when he sails from Carthage. He will have to meet her again in the underworld, and be humiliated once more.

Chapter 13
The Brink of Mystery

We can perhaps say that Aeneas is 'out of his depth' not only in his dealings with Dido but throughout much of the poem. Homer's heroes, Achilles and Odysseus, are at the mercy of the gods, but they are none the less at home in their own world; they are, in some important sense, in control of their own experience and both express themselves in superbly articulate speeches. Aeneas, we feel, is different. He does have one enormous speech, the narrative which occupies almost the whole of Books 2 and 3 (modelled of course on Odysseus' account of his adventures), but Virgil makes him stress at the start how reluctant he is to embark upon it; and this apart, he does much less talking than his Homeric models. Excluding his narrative, his longest speeches are in Book 4 (to Dido) and Book 8 (to Evander). Virgil introduces each by saying that it was short, and perhaps, given the importance of the issues involved, we may agree; each is indeed shorter than speeches by Helenus, Dido, Jupiter, Evander, Turnus and Drances. Nor are these fluent speeches: his words to Dido are painstakingly formal, and even tactless; his address to Evander (which is not meant to be strongly emotive) is stiffly diplomatic. Turnus is allowed a long speech of passionate, articulate argument on the Homeric model (11. 378-444); Aeneas is not. Instead, he is a listener, a man under instruction; he learns from dreams and visitations, from Helenus, Evander, Venus, Anchises, Creusa, Tiberinus, the Sibyl.

Aeneas has to cope with a world which has become in some ways incomprehensible; and at moments perhaps the same can be said even of us, the readers. Consider the gods. The purposes of Homer's gods may be obscure to the men and women in the poems, but they lie open to the omniscience of the poet. In the *Aeneid* this is no longer fully true. As Aeneas enters the underworld, Virgil prays to the gods that he may be permitted to speak of what he has heard and reveal things hidden in deep earth and darkness (6. 264ff.). He puts into our minds the notion that it is very difficult to say anything about such matters; of course he has to describe what Aeneas sees in the underworld, or he could not the write the book at all, but he suggests that this

63

revelation of things unseen is a special dispensation; and even so, though much is revealed, much remains unexplained.

He also gives parts of the underworld a dreamlike or uncanny feeling. We sometimes jump from one place to another with the inconsequence familiar to us in dreams. At the end, Aeneas and the Sibyl leave through the gate of ivory: where is it? how does he come to find himself near his ships as soon as he has passed through? how does he part from the Sibyl? – we are left puzzled. Similarly, we were not told anything about Aeneas' journey from the cave mouth to the underworld. 'They *were passing* in the dark through the house of Dis...' Virgil begins (6. 268); with another dreamlike jump the transition from the upper world to the realm of the dead has been made almost before we realised that it had begun.

And Virgil continues here with one of the strangest of all his similes. Normally similes are basically unlike the things with which they are compared. That may seem paradoxical, but it is in fact a fairly simple truth. When Homer says that a warrior is like a lion, the comparison is effective because in most respects a warrior differs from a lion: he does not have claws, or a tail or a mane. The unlikeness of man and lion focuses our attention on the comparatively few respects in which they are like – fierceness, courage, foam on the jaws or whatever – and thus clarifies our understanding. But Virgil's simile at this point is quite different:

> They were passing in the dark, in the lonely night, through the shadows, through the empty house of Dis and his insubstantial realm, like a journey made in the woods beneath the grudging light of a fitful moon, when Jupiter has hidden the sky in shadow and black night has stolen the colour from things.
>
> (268ff.)

Their journey in the dark was like a journey in the dark – what clarification is there in that? We are in a place where metaphor, symbol and actuality seem to be blurred and confused. The first things that Aeneas encounters are abstractions, emotions: Grief, Death, Toil, the evil Joys of the mind; for a moment we may wonder whether Virgil is describing an episode in Aeneas' adventures or a psychological state.

The significance of all this is that the underworld is not in truth a dream or a psychological state but a part of reality that may seem to us to have these elusive qualities. Virgil goes to some trouble to show us that the underworld is, within the fiction of his poem, a real place with a specific geographical location. He even feels the need to explain the lighting system: Elysium has its own sun and stars (6. 641), which is why, although underground, it is bathed in light. If the underworld were a dream, Palinurus and Dido would not, after all, still be suffering after death, and those great scenes would lose their poignancy. If the underworld were a dream, its strangenesses would not be especially interesting. Virgil's purpose is deeper and subtler: he shows us that the real experience of Aeneas includes things too mysterious for clear explanation.

It is not only in the darkness of the underworld that we may feel ourselves baffled. Virgil throws out questions, and does not give us the answers. 'Do such deep resentments dwell in divine hearts?' he asks as early as his eleventh line, after telling how remorselessly Juno persecuted the noble Aeneas. And in the last book (503ff.) he asks, 'Was it your pleasure, Jupiter, that peoples who would henceforth live in perpetual peace should clash in so great a shock?' We should be wrong to suggest that no kind of answer can be given; it is significant, though, that Virgil chooses to throw out questions in this way. It is man's lot to interrogate the divine purposes, and to get no certain reply.

Within the poem Jupiter sometimes unfolds his plans plainly, as in the first book, but his speech in Book 10, 104-13, is perhaps the most difficult passage in the entire poem. One may wonder whether Virgil would have let it stand unchanged; none the less, the terse, abrupt style shows that it is meant to be grandly oracular. Virgil wants to suggest the enigma at the heart of the divine will. Similarly, we may wonder why Neptune requires a man's life to be forfeit to him when he grants Aeneas and his men safe passage to Cumae; it seems a wish without a motive. His victim, Palinurus, is unable to cross the river Styx because he has not been buried, and the Sibyl sternly rebukes him for trying to accompany Aeneas to the other side (6. 376): 'Cease hoping to turn the gods' decree by prayer.' He is commanded to obey, not to understand; such is the lot of man.

Chapter 14
Softness and Severity

So far it may seem that the comparison with Homer shows Virgil to be darker or gloomier than his model. That would be a misleading impression, and it would be uncharacteristic of Virgil to offer such a flat and one-sided moral. We have noted that, in rough terms, the first half of the poem draws upon the *Odyssey* and the second half on the *Iliad*, but we may also say that in a sense the poem as a whole is a new *Odyssey*, for it too is a story of *nostos*. Aeneas in going to Italy is coming back to his ancient 'home', the place from which Dardanus, ancestor of the Trojans, originated; 'Here is our home, this is our fatherland,' as Aeneas tells his men (7. 122). Like the *Odyssey*, the *Aeneid* culminates in the hero's triumph in combat and his recovery of power. In some sense, possibly superficial, it cannot be gainsaid that the *Aeneid* has a 'happy ending'; the hero is victorious, he will rule in Latium, and will in due course become a god.

But there is another and perhaps more interesting way of looking at the matter. If the story of the poem as a whole shadows the *Odyssey*, it may equally be said that the tone of the poem as a whole, in its seriousness and solemnity, leans towards the *Iliad*. Besides, the influence of the *Iliad* predominates as the work proceeds; and in Book 7 when Virgil moves from what modern scholars have called the 'Odyssean' to the 'Iliadic' *Aeneid* he declares that a greater work and a greater theme now lie before him (7. 44ff.).

We have found the *Iliad* to be a bleakly tragic poem; by comparison the *Aeneid* is bound to seem more hopeful. Halfway through it threatens a horror which in the event is avoided. The Sibyl indicates to Aeneas that he will have to fight another Trojan War and tells him that a 'second Achilles' awaits him in Latium (6. 83ff.); she refers, of course, to Turnus, and we might therefore expect Aeneas to have to play the unhappy role of Hector in the *Iliad*. But events do not turn out as this prophecy would seem to imply. The war, terrible though it is, comes to a swift and decisive end; and in the last books the Homeric pattern twists round, with Turnus taking Hector's part, Aeneas that of Achilles. Moreover, Aeneas is an Achilles who does not die on the battlefield; instead, he gains a new wife, home and kingdom. And despite the Sibyl, these successes are not designed to come to us as surprises: Jupiter in the first book and Creusa in the second have foretold them.

This scheme posed Virgil a technical problem of very great difficulty. The *Iliad* can afford to end with reconciliation (of a sort) because Achilles and Priam are both tragic figures; but Achilles' nobility at the end would seem shallow were he not under the sentence of death. Virgil could not follow Homer here: lofty speeches of forgiveness and good intentions by Aeneas and Latinus would seem unbearably flat and sententious. His solution is dazzlingly original. He crowds the last thirty lines with action and ends instantly upon the death of Turnus, thus producing an ending unmatched for density, excitement and abruptness. So there is no description within the poem of reconciliation between Aeneas and his former enemies, though we know that one is about to come: once Turnus is dead, we have been told that the Trojan and Latin nations will be joined together in everlasting peace (12. 504). More important still, there is another reconciliation within the poem, between Jupiter and Juno themselves.

Juno was (unlike Venus, say) a great Roman goddess: she was one of the 'Capitoline triad', the three deities who protected the Capitol, the symbolic and sacred heart of the Roman state. So when she appears, in the poem's fourth line, the first god to be named in the *Aeneid*, as Aeneas' remorseless foe, the great obstacle to the fulfilment of Rome's destiny, we feel a dissonance; here is something which must be explained and altered before the poem can come to its conclusion. And therefore when she finally yields in the last book, and comes to accept Jupiter's plan for Rome, the effect is of a resolution long delayed. The language is sonorous, and the massive solidity of the scene conveys a sense of conclusion; and it is by thus 'tying up the loose ends' among the gods that Virgil is free to fill his last scene with speed, drama and violence. He has thereby inverted the scheme of the *Iliad*'s ending. On the surface the *Iliad*'s conclusion is slow and peaceful, but underneath nothing has changed. On the surface the *Aeneid*'s ending is abrupt and violent, but underneath everything has changed: a new order is established, and even a great goddess will change to accommodate it.

The form of the ending shapes the moral meaning. Much of what Virgil has to say is almost embarrassingly optimistic, but he is able to avoid glibness by showing us the harshness that attends the achievement of the great work. We see Turnus die, against his wish; we see Aeneas suppressing his first instinct to mercy and driving his weapon into Turnus' body to avenge the death of Pallas. It is often said that Virgil 'counts the cost' of Aeneas' and Rome's success; that is true, but it is misleading if it is taken to mean that Virgil thereby casts doubt upon the value of the final achievement. There is in fact a toughness, even a fierce splendour, to be found in other parts of the *Aeneid*. When Jupiter describes the peace which Augustus will bring, his symbolism is ferocious: Rage bound with a hundred chains, howling and dribbling blood (1. 294-6). Or take the last words of Anchises' speech in the sixth book: Rome's task will be 'to spare the conquered and beat down the proud in war' (6. 853). Roman history shows what was meant by that: mercy of a kind, maybe, but also death, enslavements and the savage rituals of the triumph. Virgil is not saying that everyone should be forgiven the moment he lays down his arms, and no Roman would for one moment have supposed him to be doing so. We should also be aware of the importance of glory to Virgil. Anchises concludes by declaring that others (that is, the Greeks) will be better at sculpture, oratory and astronomy; the Roman arts will be those of conquest and government (6. 847ff.). Virgil is not here saying (as some modern writers suppose) that the Romans must give up the arts and graces of civilization; that would be absurd, not least because Virgil was writing in the generation after Cicero had carried Latin oratory to great heights. The painful truth is rather that the Romans will essay these things, but they will never quite equal the Greek achievement in them; the comparison is in terms of glory.

The tough streak in Virgil is worth remembering when we consider a different way in which he softens Homer. Whereas the *Iliad*'s tone is tragic throughout, the *Aeneid*, though it has tragic elements, notably in Dido's case, tends rather to a lyric pathos; we have seen one example of this in Creusa's scene. The poem is flooded with a sense of loss: at the end Aeneas' own gains, great though they be, may seem to us more abstract and arid than the things he has lost: Troy, Creusa, Anchises. The second half of the poem is filled with the deaths of admirable young people: the dead Marcellus at the end of Book 6 prepares the way for the deaths of Pallas, Nisus, Euryalus, Lausus, Camilla and Turnus. There was a maiden warrior in some versions of the Troy story, Penthesilea, but the austerity of the *Iliad* has no place for her; Virgil, however, treats Camilla at length, with delicacy and affection (once more one wonders why he has ever been taken for a misogynist). The (much less successful) episode of Nisus and Euryalus in Book 9 takes the rather brutal material of the *Iliad*'s tenth book and transmutes it by adding the elements of a love story.

The dead Euryalus, with his lolling neck, is likened to a purple flower severed by a plough, or poppies drooping under the weight of rain (9. 435ff.); Pallas on his bier is compared to a soft violet or drooping hyacinth, plucked by a maiden's hand (11. 68ff.). These similes have a partial ancestry in Homer, but Virgil gives them a more languorous colour, tinged with a hint of erotic feeling.

The mournful, melancholy aspect of Virgil has been much celebrated, and little more perhaps need be said about it here except to remark that it gains much of its force from being in tension with the poet's robuster side. In the underworld Aeneas seems likely to linger with the mutilated ghost of his old comrade in arms, Deiphobus. The Sibyl presses him onward: *nos flendo ducimus horas*, 'We squander the hours in weeping' (6. 539). That might almost be a motto for the poem as a whole. On the one hand stands the impulse – humane and natural – to linger compassionately over man's suffering; but there is also the urge, no less natural and proper to humanity, to press on with vigour towards manly achievement. As Jupiter says, 'To spread glory by one's deeds, that is valour's task' (10. 468f.). Virgil's poem has a large and serious view of the world because it comprehends and values both these elements of the human spirit. If Virgil were no more than a languid aesthete, shedding soft tears over the misery of man's lot, his view of life would be, as George Orwell said of Hardy and Housman, 'not tragic, merely querulous'.

It is characteristic of Virgil to impose a severe tone, yet to temper it with a glimmer of happier things. One example of this is what might be called the motif of the lost embrace. In Book 1 it is only as she departs that Aeneas realises that the young woman with whom he has been conversing is his mother. Why, he asks, is she so cruel? why might he not have clasped her hand in his? (408ff.) That seems a rather formal gesture as between mother and son; but even this is denied him. As Creusa's ghost disappears, he tries three times to embrace her, but her form eludes his grasp, as insubstantial as sleep or the wind (2. 792-4). The three exquisite lines describing this disappointment are repeated word for word when Aeneas meets his father in the underworld (6. 700ff.): Anchises too is only a ghost and even in happy Elysium the solid comfort of contact, flesh to flesh, is denied. But in Book 8, Venus comes to Aeneas and embraces him of her own accord (8. 608ff.). The scene is not given much weight, but it gains force from its contrast with those earlier passages. It is one of the small signals by which Virgil tells us that events are flowing Aeneas' way.

Chapter 15

Landscape, History and Patriotism in the *Aeneid*

We have seen that the *Odyssey* brought landscapes into the epic poem; and Virgil, for his part, was fascinated by nature and landscape throughout his career. His *Eclogues* contain little vignettes of scenery; the *Georgics* is a profound exploration of the Italian land. In the *Aeneid* he builds upon the *Odyssey*, weaving into the fabric of his poem some of the themes that had pervaded his earlier work.

The whole *Aeneid* tells of the remnants of a people who have lost their land and their city and are seeking to replace them. It is therefore especially forceful that when we first see Aeneas and his followers, they are at sea, tempest-tossed. When the storm is stilled and the Trojans make landfall, they 'possess the longed-for shore with mighty love of the earth' (1. 171f.) – a phrase pregnant with significance. On the surface, it means that they are relieved to be alive and on dry land, but behind the superficial sense we hear a deeper import: the longing of mankind for home and soil.

Virgil depicts the harbour where the Trojans have found refuge in one of the finest pieces of landscape description ever written. It is a mere ten lines long, and some of its elements are taken from passages of the *Odyssey*, but its essence is wholly new. The harbour is a spectacular place: vast cliffs loom up towards the sky, rocks overhang a cave, the woods rustle with shuddering shade. In an earlier poet this would surely be a place of fear and horror, but for Virgil it is not; this harbour is both beautiful and safe. Here we meet a newly romantic feeling for nature: Virgil has made the discovery that the very wildness and strangeness of a landscape may be a source of pleasure and, paradoxically, of peace.

There is paradox of another kind when the Trojans reach Italy: they are strangers here, but this is also their 'ancient mother' (3. 96), since, as we have seen, it was the birthplace of their ancestor Dardanus. In a dream the river Tiber (Tiberinus) welcomes Aeneas to Italy: 'O long awaited by the soil of Laurentum and the fields of Latium' (8. 38). Virgil wants us to feel that a people's manhood and patriotism are embedded in their native earth: introducing his roll call of the Italian forces, he speaks of the 'men with whom the nurturing land of Italy blossomed even then' (7. 643f.). And he makes us freshly aware of the landscape by inviting us to see the familiar as though it were strange, by showing us the well-known Italian scene through strange eyes.

In the seventh book the Trojans sail along the coast of Latium. An essential imaginative demand of the poem is that we fancy ourselves to be Italians of Virgil's own time. That done, we find here the familiar made strange in two ways. Firstly, our own, ordinary Latium is seen through the eyes of strangers, for whom it is a new found land. But history also has an estranging effect: in Virgil's day this was one of the most populous parts of the world, with the busy port of Ostia at the Tiber's mouth. But what the Trojans see is a thick forest, with the Tiber bursting out from the woodland darkness into the sea. By travelling back in time we find that the centre of the civilised world has been transformed into a jungle.

Virgil applies his prismatic method not only to people but to places also: he shows us them in various lights, and through different pairs of eyes. We find this technique combined with his way of seeing the familiar as strange in the eighth book. The Tiber's current has been miraculously stilled, and in seven lines (90-6) Virgil describes the scene as the Trojans row up the river to the site of the future Rome. The passage seems simple. It is paratactic – that is, virtually without subordinate clauses – so that the verse drifts smoothly onwards, matching the Trojans' calm movement through the water. In reality there is much complexity here; we see the scene from several viewpoints. The first of these is our own. We Italians see the familiar stretch of water made strange in two ways: by miracle we find the notoriously turbulent Tiber made glassy and still, and by travelling into the past we find, as in Book 7, a densely populated area turned into unexplored jungle (the Trojans 'conquer the long bends', they are 'covered by trees' and 'cut through the green forest'). Then there is the Trojans' view: they are witnessing a miracle, and penetrating into the unknown. A little later we encounter the Arcadians' view, as they suddenly see a ship gliding silently through trees (Virgil chooses his words to bring out the paradox and magic of the event, 107ff.). And there is a fourth viewpoint, that of nature itself. This is the stroke of genius: the passage is flooded with words of wonder, but the wondering is attributed not to people but to the inanimate landscape:

Fig. 6. Like the Aeneid, *the Altar of Peace links the story of Rome with a celebration of the Italian land. Here the figure of a goddess represents peace and the bounty of the earth, shown in the increase of crops, flocks and herds. The goddess' identity is uncertain: she may be Peace, Earth, Ceres, Venus or Italy.*

'The waters wonder...the wood wonders...' Man and nature merge; magic and marvel flow through both alike.

Virgil's evocations of nature are not only profound and beautiful in themselves but an intimate part of his patriotic theme. Much of the second half of the poem concerns Aeneas' engagement with Italy. In the seventh book he has to pray to 'rivers still unknown' (137ff.); he is as yet a stranger. In the eighth book he meets Evander, who was also once an outsider: an exile from Greece but one who has become so assimilated into his new home that he can speak of 'we Italians' (331ff.). Entrusted to Aeneas' charge is Pallas, the son of a Greek father and an Italian mother; in his person the fusion of the alien and the native is represented. In the last book Aeneas is likened to a hound from Umbria, in the heart of Italy, and, in a very striking simile, to a mountain, Athos or Eryx or father Apenninus (753, 701ff.). This succession of mountains, in Thrace, Sicily and the centre of Italy, follow the path of Aeneas' wanderings; by the end of the poem he has become – within the imagery – part of the landscape of Italy itself. After his death he will become one of the *indigites* (12. 794); these were native Italian deities.

The poet's Italian theme helps him too with the other patriotic aspect of his project: the rule of Augustus and the imperial power of contemporary Rome. Augustus and empire were two quite separate issues, and it is a tribute to Virgil's skill in blurring this fact that in modern discussions they are quite often treated as one. He was lucky in that Augustus was indeed a formidably great figure in Roman history (which is not to say that he was necessarily attractive or sympathetic); imagine how different the poem would feel if it had been written for Claudius or Nero. None the less, Virgil faced an immense problem in fitting his patron into a poem of universal significance. Part of his answer is to deprive Augustus of all individuality or personality, to make him close to a symbol of Rome, the representative of her world-wide power; but one may still feel that there is an awkwardness here which no poet could wholly overcome.

In one place, though, Augustus seems perfectly integrated into his context in the poem: on the shield described at the end of Book 8. Virgil presents Augustus at Actium as a leader of Italians (8. 678; compare 626 and 715); that will have struck Virgil's contemporaries, who would have expected the name of Rome. In this Augustus is not entirely unlike Aeneas, who thanks to his alliance with Evander is already a leader of Italians, as Evander himself points out (8. 513).

But for the most part the passage of time turns history upside down: Aeneas leads an eastern people into battle against Italians; Augustus leads Italians against Cleopatra, whose forces are represented (or misrepresented) in oriental colours. Yet there is also a mighty continuity across the centuries: Augustus is Aeneas' direct descendant, and he carries into battle the very same gods that his ancestor brought from Troy (this is shown by 8. 679, echoing 3. 12). Thus we are shown that interplay of change and continuity which we call history. Here Virgil's ambition to write a poem which would bring together in a single vision a man and a people, the particular and the universal, myth and history, present and past is superbly achieved.

Suggestions for Further Study

1. Is there too much fighting in the *Iliad*? What shape, structure and variety are there in the battle scenes?

2. Is Hector the most sympathetic figure in the *Iliad*? Does the poem have two joint protagonists?

3. Does Odysseus become wiser in the course of his adventures?

4. Odysseus does not enter the poem that bears his name until the fifth book. What do the first four books contribute to the story?

5. Should we see Aeneas' career as a triumph of the will, or is he the passive instrument of destiny?

6. Does the second half of the *Aeneid* suggest a distaste for war?

7. Is Augustus at the centre of Virgil's poem, or is he marginal?

Suggestions for Further Reading

This is not a list of the best works on Homer and Virgil. For the most part it excludes works not in English, articles not available in book form, and works which are technical or require advanced knowledge. It merely offers a few pointers.

HOMER

Introductory works or general surveys

Both poems:

Kirk, G.S. (1962) *The Songs of Homer* (Cambridge) [thorough and judicious].

Camps, W.A. (1980) *An Introduction to Homer* (Oxford) [informative in brief compass].

Griffin, J. (1980) *Homer* (Oxford) [stylish short introduction for the general reader].

Wace, A.J.B. and Stubbings, F.H. (eds) (1962) *A Companion to Homer* (London) [compendious on the background: composition, history, archaeology].

Bowra, C.M. (1972) *Homer* (London).

Hainsworth, J.B. (1969) *Homer* (Oxford) [in the *Greece and Rome* New Surveys series, concisely assesses the state of play in Homeric scholarship].

Iliad:

Mueller, M. (1984) *The Iliad* (London) [excellent literary study].

Silk, M.S. (1987) *Homer: The Iliad* (Cambridge) [introductory but distinctive].

Schein, S. (1984) *The Mortal Hero: an introduction to Homer's Iliad* (Berkeley).

Edwards, M. (1987) *Homer: Poet of the Iliad* (Baltimore).

Odyssey:

Griffin, J. (1987) *Homer: The Odyssey* (Cambridge).

The Homeric question, oral poetry, etc.

Milman Parry's (very technical) work can be found in *The Making of Homeric Verse: the Collected Papers of Milman Parry*, ed. Adam Parry (Oxford, 1971) [the introduction (by his son) is excellent].

Page, D.L. (1955) *The Homeric Odyssey* (Oxford) and (1959) *History and the Homeric Iliad*, appendix (Berkeley) [the analyst case, set out with panache].

Parry, Adam, 'Have we Homer's Iliad?' in his *The Language of Achilles and Other Papers*, ch. 10 (Oxford, 1989) [brilliant defence of a strongly unitarian position].

Kirk, G.S. (1976) *Homer and the Oral Tradition* (Cambridge) [esp. ch. 6 (reply to A. Parry)] and the introduction to his commentary on *Iliad* Books 1-4 (see below).

Homeric values

Finley, M.I. (1954) *The World of Odysseus* (New York) [historian's view, attractively presented].

Divergent views on these vexed issues may be found in Dodds, E.R. (1951) *The Greeks and the Irrational* (Berkeley), chs 1-2 [classic study, but needs modification].

Adkins, A.W.H. (1960) *Merit and Responsibility* (Oxford), chs 1-4.

Lloyd-Jones, H. (1971) *The Justice of Zeus* (Berkeley), chs 1-2.

Rowe, C.J. 'The Nature of Homeric Morality' in *Approaches to Homer* (1983), Rubino, C. and Shelmerdine, C. (eds) (Austin) [a good adjudication of the debate between Adkins and one of his critics].

Literary studies with a more particular case to argue

Iliad:

Two outstanding works are Redfield, J.M. (1975) *Nature and Culture in the Iliad* (Chicago) and Griffin, J. (1980) *Homer on Life and Death* (Oxford).

Weil, Simone 'The *Iliad*, poem of might', in her *Intimations of Christianity Among the Ancient Greeks* (London, 1957).

Odyssey:

Austin, N. (1975) *Archery at the Dark of the Moon* (Berkeley).

Page, D.L. (1981) *Folktales in Homer's Odyssey* (Cambridge, Mass.).

Vidal-Naquet, P. 'Land and sacrifice in the *Odyssey*', in *Myth, Religion and Society*, ed. Gordon, R.L. (Cambridge, 1981), ch. 5.

Auerbach, E. (1953) *Mimesis* (Princeton) [ch. 1 analyses a passage of the *Odyssey*; relevant to Homeric narrative more generally].

Commentaries

Iliad:

On the smaller scale there is a commentary in two vols by Willcock, M.M. (London, 1978 and 1984); also his (1976) *A Companion to the Iliad* (Chicago) for those reading in translation [concise and helpful].

Macleod, C.W. (1982) commentary on *Iliad* 24 (Cambridge) is excellent; the introduction offers an interpretation of the poem as a whole.

A very large scale commentary is under way; the first two volumes, ed. Kirk, G.S., covering Books 1-8, are already published (Cambridge, 1985-).

Odyssey:

Smaller scale: Stanford, W.B. in two vols (2nd edn, London, 1959).

For those reading in translation, see Jones, P.V. *Homer's Odyssey: A Companion to the Translation of Richmond Lattimore* (Bristol, 1988).

A larger scale commentary first published in Italian is now coming out in English (Oxford, 1988-); the editors are Heubeck, A., West, S., Hainsworth, J.B., Hoekstra, A., Russo, J. and Fernandez-Galiano, M.

VIRGIL

Introductory works or general surveys

Griffin, J. (1986) *Virgil* (Oxford) [elegant short introduction for the general reader].

Quinn, K. (1969) *Virgil's Aeneid: a critical description* (London).

Camps, W.A. (1969) *An Introduction to Virgil's Aeneid* (Oxford) [sensible and useful].

Anderson, W.S. (1969) *The Art of the Aeneid* (Englewood Cliffs).

Williams, R.D. (1987) *The Aeneid* (London).

Gransden, K.W. (1990) *Virgil: The Aeneid* (Cambridge).

Other literary studies

Heinze, R. *Virgil's Epische Technik* (3rd edn, Leipzig 1915) [a classic study; a translation is to be published by Bristol Classical Press].

Johnson, W.R. (1976) *Darkness Visible: a study of Vergil's Aeneid* (Berkeley) [overwrought, but contains some admirable insights].

Otis, B. (1963) *Virgil: a study in civilized poetry* (Oxford) [interestingly develops Heinze's account of Virgil's subjectivity].

Pöschl, V. (English version 1962) *The Art of Vergil: image and symbol in the Aeneid* (Ann Arbor).

Williams, G. (1983) *Technique and Ideas in the Aeneid* (New Haven).

Gransden, K.W. (1984) *Virgil's Iliad* (Cambridge) [on Books 7-12].

Lyne, R.O.A.M. (1987) *Further Voices in Vergil's Aeneid* (Oxford).

Clausen, W. (1987) *Virgil's Aeneid and the Tradition of Hellenistic Poetry* (Berkeley).

Lewis, C.S. (1942) *A Preface to Paradise Lost* (Oxford) [opens with a beautifully written analysis of primary and secondary epic, including a chapter (reprinted in Commager; see below) specifically on Virgil].

Cairns, F. (1989) *Virgil's Augustan Epic* (Cambridge) [tends to be technical, but parts are more accessible, e.g. ch. 5].

On Dido, see Rudd, N. (1976) *Lines of Enquiry* (Cambridge), ch. 2 [shrewd and lucid; also in Harrison – see below].

Some of the best Virgilian scholarship and criticism has come in articles. There are various collections of reprinted articles:

Commager, S. (ed.) *Virgil: a collection of critical essays* (Englewood Cliffs, 1966) includes notably Lewis, C.S. on secondary epic, Knox, B. on Book 2, and two essays of general interpretation by Clausen, W. and Parry, A. [Parry's is also in his *The Language of Achilles and Other Papers* (Oxford, 1989)].

Harrison, S.J. (ed.) *Oxford Readings in Vergil's Aeneid* (Oxford, 1990) is a rich collection: 25 articles, preceded by the editor's short survey of modern scholarship.The standard is good throughout; one might pick out Rudd, N. on Dido, Solmsen, F. on Book 6, Anderson, W.S. on the second half of the poem, Fraenkel, E. on Book 7, West, D.A. on similes.

Commentaries

There is a small scale commentary in two volumes by Williams, R.D. (London, 1972-3). On the larger scale see his commentaries on Books 3 and 5 (Oxford, 1960 and 1962).

There are admirable commentaries in the same series by Austin, R.G. on Books 1, 2, 4 and 6 (Oxford, 1955 etc.).

Other commentaries: Fordyce, C.J. on Books 7 and 8 (Oxford, 1977) [very brief on the latter book]; Eden, P.T., Book 8 (Leiden, 1975); Gransden, K.W., Book 8 (Cambridge, 1976).